Getting to Know God

by

Father Eddie Doherty

MADONNA HOUSE
Combermere, Ontario

PUBLICATIONS
Canada   K0J 1L0

© Copyright February 2, 1998 Madonna House Publications. All rights reserved. No part of this book may be reproduced, stored in a retrieval system or transmitted in any form or by any means, electronic, mechanical, or otherwise, without written permission of Madonna House Publications.

Edited and compiled by: Mary Bazzett
Cover Design: Rob Huston

Special thanks to Mary Sullivan for her tireless work in selecting and extracting from the writings of Fr. Eddie Doherty.

Canadian Cataloguing in Publication Data
Doherty, Eddie 1890-1975

GETTING TO KNOW GOD

ISBN 0-921440-47-2

1. Meditations. I. Title.

BV4832.2.D63 1997   242   C97-901233-3

Madonna House Publications
Combermere, Ontario
K0J 1L0

Printed in Canada

Table of Contents

Foreword 7
Introduction 11

January
Happy New Year, God 15
Old Butch: A Success Story 18
Like a Ton of Bricks 20
The Fighting Sullivans 22
Go For It! 24
A Tender Lily 25
An Acrobat's Ante 27

February
A Family Gathering 33
Loving God Enough 38
Three Cigarettes a Day 40
Praying In Bed 41
He Lived on Eels 43
Freeing the Man Possessed 45

March
Maker of Puzzles 47
Persecutions 50
Humility 50
The Woman at the Well 51
Cleansing the Temple 56

April
Easter Parade 60
Of Easter and Liturgists 60
A Prayer of Joy 65
Fish and Taxes 68

May

The Story of Slug	72
Pistol Pete's People	77
Coming Home	78
Combermere—Temporary Heaven	80

June

More Than a Statue	86
Spring Wild Flowers	88
Not Your Average Wife	89

July

Posthole Passion	95
Where the Wild Strawberries Grow	98
Lady at the Golden Door	101
God's Humor	103

August

Belly Button Beauty	106
Fishing on the Madawaska	108
All You Need Is Love	112

September

We Are Trees	114
At the Foot of the Cross	114
Staying in the Word of God	116

October

A Rosebud and a Return	118
Autumn Glory Days	123
Listening to God	125
Seeing God's Glory	127

November

Ask For Help 129
Death 130
Favors from Martin 131
Personal Favors: From New Jersey to Harlem 136

December

Canadian Winter 140
An Advent Amethyst 142
Happy Birthday, Lord Jesus! 143

Other Books by Eddie Doherty 146

Foreword

Eddie Doherty and I lived side by side, cheek by jowl, for some twenty years, from 1955 to 1975. He occupied the large, upstairs bedroom in Madonna House—still known as Fr. Eddie's room. My bedroom was at the other end of the top floor.

Eddie's room served many purposes. It was there, for instance, that we would meet after hours. Eddie and his wife, Catherine, Father John Callahan, Father Eugene Cullinane and I would gather there in the evening. Under Catherine's leadership as the foundress of Madonna House, we would discuss the events of the day or anything else which might be percolating in that extremely fertile mind of hers. Eddie would be lying in a hospital bed, with the rest of us comfortably seated close by.

Why the hospital bed? Because Eddie had been suffering from heart trouble since 1948. He was up and down, but at that time of night, after ten o'clock, he generally was down. Catherine loved to sit by his bedside, holding his hand, as if getting her infusion of love after an extremely busy day.

Eddie and Catherine's marriage was a perfect love affair. They lived a joy and an intimacy which they knew were gifts from God. Yet when the staff of Madonna House realized they were being called to live in poverty, chastity and obedience, Eddie and Catherine agreed for the sake of the Apostolate to do the same. And their vow of celibacy, instead of diminishing their love for each other, helped it to increase by leaps and bounds. We saw it happening before our own eyes.

Eddie's room was also the haven of all sorrows. He was the ever-present, ever-loving, ever-patient and empathetic listener. His own heart had been broken several times—by his first wife Marie's death, then by his second wife Mildred's sudden and totally unexpected one. Our Lady of Sorrows (this was his favorite title for the Mother of Jesus), had mended his heart and filled it to overflowing with love for sinners and for anyone else who suffers.

When I first arrived in 1955, I would drop in once in a while to see Eddie and ask him questions about Madonna House. He surprised me constantly by responding "I don't really know. This is Katie's show."

When he had obtained permission from Bishop Bernard Sheil of Chicago to marry Catherine in 1943, the Bishop had had him kneel down, and then said, "Do you promise to live in poverty, as Catherine does?" Eddie had answered, "Yes."

"Do you promise that wherever the Apostolate is concerned, she is the director and you are a staff worker?" Now Eddie was a strong man, an independent man, a successful man, a man's man. Yet for the love of God and Catherine, he answered, "Yes." I can witness with all my strength that Eddie was totally faithful to these rather extraordinary and most difficult promises. Of course Madonna House was *their* apostolate, but in his eyes, in his heart, in his behavior, it was Katie's. He followed wherever she led.

Eddie kept on writing despite his heart problems. He wrote books and articles and edited *Restoration*, the Madonna House monthly newspaper, for several years, but his main works were to love and to suffer. Every week or two he spent several days mostly in bed, due to his heart condition. The pain of it much weakened him. Never once did I hear him complain. Rather, he would look at the statue of Our Lady of Sorrows standing on his bedside table and say, "She must want something." He knew how to offer up his pain to God, through Our Lady.

Who knows what would have happened to Catherine and to Madonna House without Eddie's love, prayer and pain? To me, he was definitely another St. Joseph, supporting Catherine his wife, and our director of priests, Father Callahan, in whose priesthood we saw Jesus among us. For the rest of the staff, he personified the Holy Spirit, the Consoler.

In those early days, Madonna House was considered an unusual entity within the Catholic Church. It wasn't common for lay people, rather than members of religious orders or priests, to be involved in the sorts of apostolates Madonna House staff were involved in and it also certainly wasn't usual for men and women to be living together in celibate community. Bishop William Smith might have had doubts about this strange new spiritual family that was growing in his diocese, but he felt reassured that Eddie Doherty was a part of it.

Today Madonna House has official status within the Catholic Church as a public association of the faithful. Over the past fifty years it has flourished and spread, and now has field houses throughout the world. Yes, Our Lady of Combermere and her Son worked out things very well. Through Catherine and Father Eddie, they established a house of love, a holy family in another Nazareth, one called Madonna House.

—Father Émile Brière
Priest of Madonna House

Introduction

"Go through that stuff and patch me up a story. This is the most important story you'll ever write.

"You'll write your best story with a pair of scissors and a bottle of paste. All I want from your typewriter is a hundred-word lead to tie all the clips together."

Those were the words of Walter Howey, Eddie Doherty's first boss at the *Chicago Tribune*, assigning him to write a breaking news story on the assassination of Archduke Francis Ferdinand of Austria on the eve of World War I. Eddie rose to the occasion. "All afternoon I read and clipped and pasted," he recalled. "My pulses pounded and I felt a glow of pride all through me. I hadn't written this story. I'd only assembled it. I'd merely strung a lot of pearls together. But what a wondrous necklace I had made!"

This book is a different kind of "cut and paste" job, this time using Eddie's "pearls" assembled by this reporter. It's the most dramatic, most colorful, most important topic he ever wrote about—the awesome story of God and what God is like. Not in theological jargon, but in everyday, common English, the way Eddie wrote and spoke.

Eddie was top notch, a crackerjack reporter and a writer with sass and verve. His writing could wring tears out of cynical, veteran editors.

He learned his craft in his home town of Chicago, where he worked for the *Chicago Tribune*. His formal education consisted of three years in a Servite monastery in Granville,

Wisconsin. His informal schooling came from newspaper reporting. Working eventually for the *Sun* (which later became the *Sun-Times*) and later for the *New York Daily Mirror* and *Liberty Magazine*, Edward J. Doherty covered the biggest news stories of his day, everything from the Lindbergh baby kidnapping to the Rose Bowl, from the antics of gangsters like Al Capone to miraculous healings attributed to a saint.

At age twenty-four, Eddie married his childhood sweetheart, Marie Ryan. Their four-year marriage, which produced a son, Eddie Jr., ended with the early death of Marie in the influenza epidemic of 1918. Her death embittered Eddie toward God and he left the Catholic Church in which he was raised.

Soon after, Eddie met and married Mildred Frisby, another newspaper reporter. They had one son, Jack Jim, who contracted polio and was left with a lifelong leg impairment. When Mildred died in a freak accident in 1939, Eddie was left a widower for the second time. In the aftermath of his grief, he returned to the Catholic Church.

While on assignment for *Liberty Magazine*, he met Catherine de Hueck, a Russian baroness. She was working with the poor in Harlem in a Catholic apostolate called Friendship House. The romantic Irishman fell in love with the blue-eyed, blonde Catherine and the two eventually were married in 1943.

Together, they came to Combermere, Ontario in 1947 and founded Madonna House, a Catholic lay group that now has about two hundred members, with twenty-two field houses serving the poor around the world.

When Madonna House members agreed to live in poverty, chastity and obedience, Eddie and Catherine agreed to do the same. Like the rest of the staff, they lived by charitable donations, including food and second-hand clothing. They lived in obedience to their spiritual director. They also lived apart in celibate chastity. They began this unusual arrangement in 1955.

In 1969, Eddie was ordained a Catholic priest in the Melkite rite (which allows married clergy), finally fulfilling a lifelong dream that had begun in the Wisconsin monastery.

Father Eddie Doherty died in 1975 at the age of eighty-five, leaving behind a life's worth of newspaper and magazine articles, a number of pamphlets and books, and even Hollywood movie scripts. But it was his last years, after he married Catherine and came to Madonna House, that produced what Eddie personally said was his biggest, most exciting story. It was the story of God working in people's lives.

Eddie maintained that his best reporting "beat" was to cover God. He even titled one of his books *I Cover God* and wrote it as a series of letters, addressed directly to the Almighty.

This book begins where his others left off. *Getting to Know God* is the result of assembling "pearls" from Eddie's numerous published articles and books, as well as unpublished material from transcripts of homilies he gave, plus a series of interviews about his colorful life. It all adds up to a deep love story, filled with several lifetimes of adventure, pain and joy. It is a story teeming with life. It is the love story of God and man.

If you want to get to know God, à la Eddie, open this book and begin. Say a wee prayer, enjoy Eddie's Irish wit and wisdom, and get to know the most fascinating, never-ending Lover of all time: God.

—Mary Bazzett
Editor

January

Happy New Year, God

January 1

It was Saturday evening and the home town had won a tremendous football victory. The city danced with liquid jubilee.

The restaurant we found was crowded. My friend Gene had passed the doctor's examinations and we wanted a fairly decent dinner to celebrate his new lease on life. We stood outside the restaurant doorway, not quite certain we wanted to go in. If we couldn't find room inside, we would mosey on.

Just as we were getting ready to leave, a Good Samaritan waved to us from inside and made us welcome.

"I'm having some trouble," he confided and smiled as if we were old friends of his and could understand and sympathize. "Too many waiters are football fans. They didn't show up. There are plenty of tables still vacant, though, if you don't mind waiting."

He was a warm, charitable, hospitable man. He seemed sincere, so we said we'd stay and wait. He thought that was wonderful of us and sent some cocktails to our table "on the house."

Some of the glow faded when we looked at the prices on the menu. We wanted to get up and go. But charity trapped us, held us. We could not be discourteous.

There was but one thing to do. That was to order the "specialty," which seemed to be the only bargain on the printed bill of fare.

It would have been a bargain at any price, for it brought God close to me.

"Relax," Gene said. "It seems to me we were brought here for some good reason. We have enough money. We have plenty of time. And we have something to celebrate, just like these football fans. God wants us to enjoy this."

It was a sort of nightclub. The tables were close to each other. We could hear what everybody around us was saying. They were young. They looked prosperous and happy. They were loud and drank more than they ate. Their drinks were of all colors. There was a jazz orchestra and a blonde singer with a pleasant voice. We sipped and waited and ordered.

Lord, you know we have some wonderful cooks at home. You also know that we seldom eat anything rich or expensive. You know how I felt about those hors d'oeuvre, particularly the anchovies, those lovely morsels that put such bitter salt joy in my mouth. You know my stand in regard to mushrooms and filet mignon and wine in my soup. (I am for it!)

The atmosphere of the place changed with the coming of the hors d'oeuvre. It was almost like being in a cathedral.

I became aware of you, God.

I became aware that you had always loved me, even when I was far away from you.

Strange!

The man with his back to us, who kept ordering a double rye with ginger ale every few minutes, talked to himself aloud. He had won $100 on the game and was going to drink it all down. "Waiter—another double rye—where's the waiter?"

The thin young man on our left introduced his girl to everybody. "Mr. Horwitz, my future wife, Anna." One man said, "Anna! May you be happy always, Anna."

The singer sang. The musicians played. The diners dined and sipped and talked and shouted and flirted. I heard and saw everything and everyone.

I was absorbed in talking to you, God, yet aware of all that was happening around me. I became aware, too, that this was not the first extraordinary dinner you had arranged for me. On the contrary!

I realized, for the first time, that you had been feeding me all my life; even when my nourishment was but the rich, warm milk of my mother. Day after day, wherever I was, whatever I had done, you had attended me, watched over me, provided for me. No matter whether I was good or bad, you loved me!

Your Son taught us to pray to you: "Our Father, who art in heaven." You had been a good Father to me—but what scant attention I had paid to you!

Often I had said grace before and after meals. But usually I said the words mechanically; with no more fervor than a busy man dictating letters. "Dear sir,... in regard to your shipment of the nineteenth, it was gratefully received. Yours very sincerely,... "

Until that moment I had never been quite conscious that you gave me every meal of my life. I had never really thanked you. Yet, you kept showering me with your love. How amazing that you love us, God! And how tragic that so few of us have any idea of your love for us!

Most of us were brought up in the belief that you are a miser, a tyrant, a God of anger and jealousy and vengeance, a greedy Deity who wants everything we have and who will send us to hell if we hold back anything at all. You are pictured as Infinite Selfishness, when all you want for yourself is our poor human love!

I felt very close to you, God, dining on filet mignon and mushrooms. How is it that I seldom feel close to you in church, yet I feel love for you in a noisy dining room? I guess that's how we're made. Feelings are not important. Intentions are.

My intentions are good, Lord. Make them better.

In that overcrowded, hoyden nightclub restaurant, surrounded by people seeking to be happy, I tried to make up to you—with a few minutes of pure love—for my long lifetime of ingratitude and neglect and sin!

But I gave you only a few minutes, against a lifetime of your unceasing love and care!

Let me spend all year loving you, God. Let me love you, Lord, from now on, not in my usual tepid, phlegmatic, stupid way, but fervently, as the saints love you.

Happy New Year, God.

Old Butch: A Success Story

Back in the early thirties, I was at the top of my trade as a newspaperman. Before I quite realized what had happened, the *New York Daily Mirror* was advertising me all over New York as "The Star Reporter of America," and the "highest-paid reporter in the United States."

My pictures were on all the newsstands, on the sides of the delivery trucks and on billboards and shanties and barns and ash cans. Whole page ads. Half page ads. Plain and fancy ads. Black and white ads, colored ads, and posters.

I was glad of one thing, that my father, Old Butch, saw those ads before he died and that he found them not at all ridiculous. They were proof to him that I'd reached the top, as long ago he had decreed I must do. They made him prouder of me than ever—and my father, a Chicago policeman, was proud enough before. When Columbia made a Class G picture out of my book *Broadway Murders,* my father went to see it at least ten times. And each time he vowed it was the finest movie ever made.

I wrote the life of Jack "Legs" Diamond, the clay-pigeon of gangland. I wrote the life story of a rum-runner, and the life and loves of a burglar, as well as many other stories.

While I was still a shining star Old Butch died suddenly. We went to Chicago for the funeral, and I learned my father's stature. For two days the house was crowded with his friends. The mighty of Chicago, and the humble. The rich. The poor. Cops. Firemen. Letter carriers. Priests. Shopkeepers. Kids. Bank presidents. Politicians. Newspapermen. They filled every room.

They overflowed into the backyard, and filled it. They cluttered up the front yard, and the front steps. Night and day there were hundreds and hundreds of them coming and going and standing about and talking. And such talk!

"The first time I saw Old Butch I was reporting to him for duty. I took off my hat. 'Where the hell do you think you are?' he yelled. 'In church? Put on your hat.' I thought he was the hardest guy in the world. I'm telling you I was scared. Me, a cop. My knees shook. But after I knew him ..."

"Acting captain! That guy broke in more good cops than any big shot on the force. He could have been a full captain, for five thousand bucks. You should have heard him talk to the guy who made him that proposition. Sure he could of got the dough from the brewery—but he wouldn't. Not Butch. Too honest."

"'Wild Jimmy' we used to call him. Because, whenever he had to throw a young kid in the can he'd go on a tear. 'Wild Jimmy!' I'll bet he spent half his life getting kids out of trouble, and getting drunk because they got themselves back into it."

Teddy Beck, my old boss, drew me aside. "At last I've seen a successful man," he said. "There he lies. He never made any money. He wasn't famous. Yet everybody knew him and loved him, and went to him for favors. He was an honest man. He was a happy man. He had work he loved and he died in harness. He lived long enough to see all his children grown up and to be proud of them. I'd call him a success."

My wife, Mildred, wormed her way through the crowd as Beck left me. "There's a little boy outside I want you to see," she whispered.

He was just a child as I must have been at six or seven, puny and pale, with innocent, wondering eyes. "Is your grandpop dead?" he asked. I nodded. "My grandpop is dead too. And he was a fine man, just like your grandpop. Only nobody comes to bring him flowers. And nobody comes to pray for him, like they do for your grandpop. And he was such a good man!"

Mildred burst into tears and caught the boy to her.

"We'll come," she said. "And we'll bring flowers. And we'll pray for him too."

Across the street and around the corner the other man lay, an aged Pole in a cheap wooden coffin, all alone in a bare clean room in the basement. There was a rosary in his hands, as there was in my father's. The crucifix looked down on him as it did on Old Butch; and the candles shone on him with the same light. There were too many flowers in my father's house. We took half of them across the street and around the corner, and banked them about the wooden casket. And we knelt and prayed.

"My grandpop will be very glad," the boy said as we left. "and maybe he'll meet your grandpop in heaven, and they'll be friends."

"Yes," Mildred said, "all people are friends in heaven. They'll be friends."

Like a Ton of Bricks

All my life as a reporter I'd seen young people in trouble, especially young men. I'd seen kids standing before a judge, pleading guilty to this and that, getting ten to twenty years. I'd seen them hang. I'd seen them drinking too much, stealing cars and cracking up. They'd be fished out of rivers and lakes, clinging to girls, in alleys, in gangs, and so forth. I'd seen them go away to war, seen them hanging around bars overseas.

But young people today can be very wonderful too. They have an intelligence my generation didn't. They have a real spark of ambition, a determination that's very wonderful. And the kids who came to Madonna House also had a sense of morality which I admired, especially in the boys.

A few years after Madonna House began, we started to get this type of boy and girl. They came here to "do something for God," as they put it. It was amazing. Here were dedicated people who wanted to work, not part-time for God, but all the time. They wanted to give him their whole lives.

My wife, Catherine, will tell you that I love only the girls, but that's crazy. I have as much regard for the boys, or even more, because they are so darn good. They're different than the average kid. They have more sense, more ability, and a decency that defies conventions and everything else. There's an inherent holiness about them that's just astonishing!

The kids here at Madonna House are young people in their twenties and thirties. It amazes me that they should have this moral attitude, this tremendous, decent wish to be close to God and to work for him. They want to give God what they have.

I remember at the old Friendship House, the young men talked about God like they were very close to him. That startled me. The people I knew never talked about God. We kept him in our pockets. Maybe we had a rosary hidden away some place, but we never took it out in public. We were ashamed to talk about God. You'd almost blush if somebody said the word Christ, unless he was swearing. But there were kids in Friendship House who openly talked about God or Our Lady or the doctrines of the Church. They not only talked about them, they explained them—very beautifully and simply! It's amazing what that does to you when you hear it.

Through that, I began to see what it means to be a lay person. I started to learn about the lay apostolate. You can talk to priests all you want and they can tell you profound things, beautiful things, but you expect it of priests. But take a man who can go out and have a drink with you in a bar, or can walk your legs off or build a cabin or a boat or any darn thing you ask him to, a big powerful brute of a man, and he talks so simply about God and Our Lady. Bang! That hits you like a ton of bricks! Then you see the power of the laity.

The power of the laity is something most people don't seem to realize they have. But they'll realize it later, as they go along. It's something simple and direct, with no Roman collars, no habits, nothing of the sort.

The Fighting Sullivans

I found out the power of the laity when I was in Hollywood, of all places. I was out there to write the script for the movie "The Fighting Sullivans."

The Sullivans were five brothers who enlisted together in the Navy and who served on the same ship together. They died together in November, 1942. They were killed in action on the U.S. cruiser Juneau. It was torpedoed in the battle off Guadalcanal.

I was sent by the *Chicago Sun* to interview the parents of the sailors, who lived in Waterloo, Iowa.

When I went into their home, there was a picture of the Sacred Heart of Jesus on the wall. It was one of those old coloured prints, a chromolithograph, with a lot of blood, not very well done. As I was leaving the house after talking to the Sullivans about their five sons, Mrs. Sullivan looked up at the picture of Christ, pointed to it, and said, "He had five wounds too."

I built my story on those five young wounds, those five meaningful Christian words. Months later, the *Catholic Digest* reprinted my story. Somebody in Hollywood read it and said, "That's the way we'll make the movie, and that's the guy who will write it for us."

A movie producer in Hollywood phoned asking me to come out there and do the work for him. I hung up the phone. I was in love with Catherine and I was pursuing her in Chicago at the time. I had no intention of leaving the city—even for big money. An author can be as coy as a woman, saying no. I wasn't playing. I meant it.

But Our Lady made the producer call again and again, always with a little more color, a little more bait on his fish hook. I kept saying no.

Eventually the voice of destiny asked, "Well, how much money do you want?" Our Lady put a fancy figure in my mind; and for a moment I was glad. This time, I was certain, Hollywood would hang up on me.

But the voice said, "All right. How soon can you come?" Which proves that even the wiliest and most reluctant of fish can be caught. I had hooked myself fast to that shining and repulsive bait. It was no use to struggle. I had named my price. I had sold myself. I was Hollywood's speckled trout.

A small delegation met me in Los Angeles and escorted me to the producer's office. There I found I was a fish indeed, and perhaps the strangest ever captured in those waters. I was something between a celebrity and a freak. I was not a newspaperman or reporter. I was not an author of books and magazine articles. I was "A Catholic Author."

Maybe something like St. Augustine or St. Thomas Aquinas. Or St. John of the Cross. "But, you know—modern! Oh, distinctly modern. Smokes cigarettes, and cigars, and a pipe. Likes Scotch whiskey. Ain't wearing sack cloth and ashes. Looks tough enough to sock a guy. But Catholic! Absolutely pure Catholic! Fantastic, huh?"

It was impossible to do anything about the Sullivans until I had answered scores of queries about the Catholic faith. It was impossible to work in that office, even for an hour, without having to talk to some spellbound newcomer about priests and nuns, celibacy, chastity, the Pope, infallibility, baptism, circumcision, sin, Satan, heaven, hell, purgatory, limbo, the Vatican, and why some priests run away and marry nuns.

Almost every night, the producer, or the director, or the press agent took me some place for Scotch and Scripture. Everybody bought a round of drinks. Everybody but me. I was the guest. And I was the entertainer. All I had to do was drink and talk.

Before the Sullivan project was finished, I realized something. What I was saying to all those people clustered around me, I was saying to myself. And what I kept saying, in many different ways, was a simple truth: "If you want to be happy, follow God's will, not your own. If you really want to know God's will, he'll let you know what it is."

Go For It!

How tremendously important lay people have become, in our barbaric age! How vital it is for lay people to make themselves as holy and as zealous as any priest or nun, and to work as hard to spread the faith!

The missionaries who brought the faith to our shores are gone; only their bones, perhaps, remain in our soil. But thousands of lay people are carrying on their work. They are grouped together in some places; in other places they are working alone. They are fasting, praying, doing penances of many kinds, spreading the names of Jesus and Mary, giving Christ to all. To do this, how vital it is for each lay man and woman to become a great saint!

Truly, God raises up saints in each age for his own purposes. This is an age of indulgence, of luxury, softness, comfort and ease—ease of body, ease of morals, ease of principles, ease of almost everything but conscience. This is an age that needs the example of saints! This is the time for the laity to know its role.

"You are the Church," Pope Pius XI said, "you Catholic lay people. You must not consider the Church as the pope, the bishops, and the priests, with yourselves as a sort of outer fringe.... You are the Church ... just as my hands are my body.... It is only through you that the Church can adapt herself to the changing conditions in the world.... Go forth to conquer the world again for Christ!"

The people have gone forth, especially those dedicated to Christ through Mary, his mother. They have gone forth to conquer and to die. Many have died, as gloriously as the martyrs under Nero and other tyrants throughout history. Those tyrants continue today, in various parts of the world, and so do the activities of both priests and many lay people, some of whom, even today, are martyrs for Christ and his Church.

A Tender Lily

St. Agnes
January 21

A young lay woman who died for her faith was St. Agnes, whose name in Greek means "pure." She was thirteen years old when she died in Rome in the year 304 or 305, during the emperor Diocletian's persecutions of the Christians. Here Eddie describes her martyrdom.

Agnes stood before the tribunal of the prefect, innocent and sweet before the judge, as virginally pure as the white flowers in her hair. She was wearing her hair loose. It was unshorn, the symbol of virginity. It hung below her waist, in gleaming waves.

Agnes was smiling.

The judge gazed on her a long time; then at the guards who had brought her, tremendous brutes standing on either side of her.

"Why was she not fettered?" he asked.

"She does not need it, she walks so readily," came the reply, "and she is so young!"

"But she is as obstinate as the oldest. Put manacles on her hands at once."

The executioner selected a pair as light and small as he could find, and placed them around her wrists. Agnes playfully, and with a smile, shook her hands. The irons fell clattering at her feet.

"They are the smallest we have, sir," said the softened executioner; "one so young ought to wear other bracelets."

"Silence!" rejoined the exasperated judge. To the prisoner, he said, in a blander tone, "Agnes, I pity you. I desire, if possible, to save you. Think while you have time. Renounce the false and pernicious maxims of Christianity, obey the emperor's imperial edicts, and sacrifice to the gods."

"It is useless," Agnes replied, "to tempt me longer. My resolution is unalterable. I despise your foolish and false divinities. I shall continue to love and serve the one living God."

She raised her voice in prayer: "Eternal Ruler, open wide the heavenly gates. Blessed Christ, call to you my soul that cleaves to you; a victim dedicated to you first by virginal consecration, and now by martyrdom."

"I'm wasting time," said the impatient prefect, who saw symptoms of compassion rising in the multitude. "Secretary, write the sentence. We condemn Agnes, for contempt of the imperial edicts, to be punished by the sword. Let it be carried into effect here, and at once!"

Agnes raised her eyes to heaven, then calmly knelt. She drew her silken hair forward over her head, and exposed her neck to the blow. The spectators were stirred. Even the judge seemed to be shocked at his own words. The executioner, trembling with emotion, could not raise his sword.

Agnes knelt in her white robe, her head inclined, her arms modestly crossed upon her bosom, her golden locks hanging almost to the ground veiling her features. She was lovely and young, like some rare plant whose slender stalk, white as the lily, bent with the luxuriance of its golden blossoms.

The judge angrily reproved the executioner for his hesitation. The executioner passed the back of his rough left hand across his eyes, then raised his sword. The next moment, flower and stem were lying, scarcely displaced, upon the ground.

* * *

The persecution of the Christians continued. Like one of those rolling storms that go over half the world, visiting various countries with ravaging energy, simultaneously overshadowing them all, so did the persecution wreak its fury first on one country, then on another, destroying everything Christian, passing from Italy to Africa, from Upper Asia to Palestine and Egypt. It left no place in actual peace, but hung above the entire empire.

A succession of tyrants and oppressors blew the storm clouds this way and that. Diocletian, Galerius, Maximinus, and Licinius in the East, Maximian and Maxentius in the West, allowed the Christians no rest.

And yet the Church increased in numbers, prospered, defied the world, the flesh and the devil. Even as the persecution went on without ceasing for nearly fifteen years in Rome, and longer in other parts of the world, so did Christ's kingdom on earth continue to grow. The greater and more poisonous the pagan hate, the greater and more healing grew the Christian love. Hate cannot conquer love. Hate exhausts itself with its own fever, and dies in exhaustion and defeat. Love is indestructible, unconquerable, immortal.

It was in the year 313 that Constantine, Emperor and convert to Christ, having defeated Maxentius, gave full liberty to the Church.

One may imagine the joy and gratitude of the Christians at this great change. It was like the coming forth of the inhabitants of a city decimated by plague, when the infection has ceased. Timid at first, then more courageous, they ventured forth. The Church was soon in motion to bring out all the resources of her beautiful forms and institutions; and either the existing basilicas were converted to her uses, or new ones were built on the most cherished spots of Rome.

One of the new basilicas was built by the princess Constantia, daughter of the Emperor Constantine. Before she was a Christian, she had come to the tomb of St. Agnes, begging to be cured of a virulent ulcer. She went away healed. Completely cured. Hence, the princess erected a basilica at Agnes's tomb. And she became a Christian.

An Acrobat's Ante
St. John Bosco
January 31

St. John Bosco used any means he could to bring boys to God. His sense of humor, his wisdom, his writing, and, occasionally, even his acrobatic prowess all came into play. Here Eddie recounts one such incident.

A professional acrobat had made the mistake of working close to the Jesuit church on a Sunday afternoon when John Bosco happened to be leading a large group of boys to catechism lessons.

With his blaring trumpet and gaudy costume, the young man was attracting a crowd; and a number of John's boys thought they would rather remain near the acrobat's stall than continue to the church.

"But this man has very little to show you," John objected—loudly enough for the acrobat to overhear. "I could beat him myself, at anything he might name."

John was short of stature for the time; in fact he looked like a small boy dressed as a young man. The acrobat might not have been so contemptuous if this boy had been taller, but to have a small boy despise him was too much.

"I heard that, young fellow," he said. "You should be more careful. I might make you eat those words."

"Sometimes words are good to eat," John answered softly. "I meant what I said. If I beat you in running, or jumping, or any other sport you name, you must quit bothering people who want to go to church on Sunday. Do you accept my challenge?"

"Sure," the acrobat said with a wide grin. "But who's talking? You or your money?"

John's grin was equally wide.

"What is the wager?" he asked.

"First, we'll race. Twenty lire to the winner. Let's see your twenty."

John had no money. But his friends had.

"Here's five of it," one of them shouted. "Here's two more," said another. "I got ten," a third exclaimed. "That makes seventeen. Who's got the rest?" Three other boys held up their hands. Three loud voices shouted, "I got it here."

Those boys were betting on a sure thing. They had often seen John Bosco run. They would have told you he could give sprinting lessons to the fastest rabbits.

A stake-holder was found and the money paid into his excited palms. John agreed to meet the acrobat Thursday, which was a holiday. Then he and his boys went on to church.

On Thursday the route for the race was determined—through the town of Chieri. An enormous crowd cheered for their favorite and the race began. But within a few minutes those who favored the professional had quit cheering. John had permitted him to get a long start, then had passed him, and left him far behind.

The acrobat stopped, conceded defeat, and called off the race.

"After all," he said, "I know I'm not as fast on my feet as I should be. I am not in running shape either. If it were a jump now—a broad jump—it would be different. Forty lire says I can outjump you. What about the river? Care to leap it with me, or do you think you might fall in?"

John grinned and put forty lire in the stake-holder's hands. Everybody went to the river and selected a portion neither too wide nor too narrow. But it was a nasty place for this sort of contest, for there was a crumbling low wall thrusting itself up from the opposite bank.

A man could break a leg on that wall. He could even break his neck. And certainly it was easy for one to fall backward into the river, supposing he succeeded in leaping the space but did not land exactly right.

"You go first," John said, bowing to his adversary.

"Frightened?" the latter asked. "Watch this. Here goes your forty lire!"

He took off without apparent effort. He made a beautiful jump and landed, lightly and gracefully, where he had intended, on the narrow bit of sod this side the wall.

"Come on over and visit," he called to John.

John obliged. But he didn't stop this side of the wall. He cleared that obstruction entirely. When he turned around to face the acrobat, he could look down on him. He was much higher up the bank!

The tumbler was shocked and humbled. He was also not a little enraged. To be beaten by a soft-speaking little Sunday School boy—and to have been robbed of sixty hard-earned lire—he could not endure that. There must be some way he could get back his lost prestige and his lost money.

But he couldn't think of any contest at the moment. Therefore he said eagerly, "You name it. Any sport. And I'll beat you. Eighty lire this time."

"What about the magic stick?" John said calmly. "I saw you do it once. You were not bad at it, either."

The acrobat was almost grateful to the boy. The magic stick, of course. But what a nerve this chump had to think he could beat the master of that trick!

"Eighty lire," he said. "The magic stick."

John held up the stick for all to see. He put his hat on it, made the hat spin with a movement of his fingers. Then he made the stick jump from his palm to the tip of his fingers, then to his forearm, then to his shoulder, then to his chin, then to his nose, and finally to his forehead. Thence it started back, still spinning, until it had reached his palm.

The acrobat found himself crouching behind a grave doubt. He couldn't beat this boy. John had done the trick perfectly. The only thing possible was to do as well, and then to hope the boy would make a mistake on the retrial. But, he had to ask himself, would he be able to make that stick behave? It was a long time since he had used this trick. He began to doubt himself.

He got the stick, spinning prettily, as far as his nose. But that was as far as he could manage. It slipped. He caught it, and flung it pettishly to the pavement.

"Well," he said, "all this is baby stuff. Let's go in for something hard. That elm over there, for instance. We'll climb that. For a hundred lire. Whoever manages to get highest in that tree takes the money."

This time he didn't say, "Are you afraid?" or make any sarcastic remarks. He was almost begging John to give him a chance to win back some of his money—just a hundred lire of it.

John hesitated, sensing the other's feelings. Undoubtedly that hundred lire was all the cash he had.

The acrobat misread John's hesitancy. He thought the boy was frightened at last. It heartened him.

When John nodded, the man tore off his coat and vest, and began to climb upward as though he were part squirrel. Before the crowd realized it, he had gained the very top of the elm, and he was being swung right and left by the wind.

Nobody could help but applaud—and feel sorry for Johnny Bosco.

They felt sorry because that branch on which the acrobat clung would never be the same again. It was near to breaking. It had lost its elasticity. Even if John managed to get high enough to touch it—and that was a dangerous thing to do, seeing what a strain had already been placed upon it—it would not take him up as high as the acrobat had been.

Even those of John's company of friends who were present felt that John had lost.

John was cheerful. And confident. He got to the top as quickly as his rival, it seemed to the silent crowd. He reached the branch the acrobat had bent—purposely or because he couldn't help it. But he could not go an inch higher! The branch had a downward slant. John would have to straighten it, then bend it upward, and then climb up to its very end if he wished to beat the tumbler. And, of course, that was impossible.

They gasped. Johnny hadn't let that injured branch interfere with his victory. He had swung his body upwards until he was standing upside down, his feet waving high above the tallest twigs around him. He held the position a long, long moment, smiling at those down below him. Not even a bird could get that high and still stay in the tree.

Is it any wonder the town of Chieri never forgot that boy?

"You covered yourself with glory," a friend gushed, overtaking him in the market place that evening, "and won enough money to keep you eating regularly for weeks."

John shrugged. Glory? Who wanted such a transitory and intangible thing, except for God? Who wanted money? Who wanted to gorge himself on food? It was true, he had spent some of the wager money on a feast for himself and his friends. But, as usual, he had managed to mortify his appetite.

He had also managed to give back a lot of money to the guest of honor, the acrobat. There were a few liras left for this family and that, and for the purchase of leather and wax and heavy wool cloth. Now he could fix little Tony Sopaldi's shoes, and patch up Dominic Garaldi's coat.

The best thing was that the tumbler would no longer try to compete with God on Sunday in Chieri. He would also, probably, perceive that a boy, or a grown man, need not be irreligious to excel in anything. He might even realize, some day, that the closer one is to God, the easier it is to borrow from God all one needs—in speed, agility, deftness, skill, courage, wisdom, or any sort of power.

Glory? Glory belonged only to God. A man was a fool even to seek for it.

One sought first the kingdom of heaven—and all things were provided for his needs.

February

It's February, and the mercury still goes to thirty below every night. Or lower. Maybe it is digging down to that ground hog we read about. The one who got frightened of his shadow and dealt us six weeks more of winter.

The pipes freeze and thaw, freeze and thaw.

The sun comes up in glory after the long cold night, and the mercury climbs at amazing speed. Sometimes twenty degrees in less than an hour. By noon it will have passed the freezing mark. Then a man can go out to the wood pile—some other man—and carry in all the fuel he needs for the grate and the range, without bothering to put on heavy gloves.

A Family Gathering
The Presentation
February 2

And when the day came for them to be purified as laid down by the Law of Moses, Mary and Joseph took Jesus up to Jerusalem to present him to the Lord.
(Lk 2:22-24)

Outside the Temple gates there is the chaffer of many tongues, the smell of animals and fowls, the changing of money, the business of the world.

Within the Temple there is peace, the fragrance of incense and of prayer, the hushed footsteps of the priests, the coo of a pigeon, the bleat of a snow-white lamb beneath the sacrificial knife.

St. Joseph and Our Lady enter quietly, humble people, poorly dressed, with the dust of a long hot road upon their garments. Joseph has an offering of doves in his right hand; and Mary, in a fold of her blue robe, carries the Hope of the World.

They are lowly people, yet exalted above all humankind. They have talked with angels, and heard their voices singing. Mary, a virgin, has borne the Son of God, and they have held him in their arms and kissed him.

The glory of the Annunciation is still in Our Lady, and the overshadowing of the Holy Spirit—how could she have endured such divine rapture, this sixteen-year-old girl?—and the wonder of Elizabeth's greeting; and the feel of the Child in her womb, growing with her blood and stirring in his sweet retreat; and the miraculous birth of the Baby in the stable at Bethlehem; and the first deep look into his eyes; and his first smile; and the first tugging of his tiny mouth upon her breast.

Joy sings in all her veins, untarnished, undimmed, undiluted by any thought of fear or sorrow. And the greatest of joys awaits her, for she has come to present her Child to his Father!

Like any mother taking her first-born home, she comes to show him off with pride, in her old home. For an old tradition has it that this Temple was her childhood home, that here her mother and father gave her up to God. Here she was raised; here she learned of God and of the Scriptures. Here bright angels came to gossip with her of the Lord. Here she met and married Joseph.

This is the house of her Father, the great Lord God Almighty. This is the home of her Spouse, the Holy Spirit.

In a moment, her Father and her Spouse will look upon her Son. And he on them! A family gathering unparalleled in heaven or on earth; a situation created by divine omnipotence before the morning star; a moment scarce bearable even to the dominations and the thrones. They are holding their breath in fear and awe.

Mary and Joseph are standing before the altar, and the priest has come in his immaculate white robes; but there is neither awe nor fear in Mary or in Joseph. There is only sublime happiness, intolerable joy.

I am chilled, remembering what is about to happen next. I call to her, "O Mother, don't be so happy. It breaks my heart to see you so. Prepare yourself for your first sorrow. A knife is reaching for your heart!"

She does not hear.

The ritual has been finished. The birds have been offered up, and their blood spilled toward the Holy of Holies. The priest is walking fast away, unaware of the miracle he has helped to bring about.

And Simeon is coming, little gold bells tinkling on the hem of his robe.

Simeon is seamed and slow and bent with the weight of the onyx stones on his shoulders and the breastplate of jewels hanging on its golden chains. Little gusts of air, stirred by the feeble motions of his head and the shaking of his hands, ripple his white beard.

His eyes are filmed with weariness and age and longing —longing for the serenity of the grave his life has earned, and for the sight of Israel's salvation. His lips are thin and bloodless, and ever in motion, shaping little prayers. Yet there is beauty in him, and majesty, and a great benevolence. The smell of incense and lilies walks with him, and wisdom guides him; for he is filled with the Holy Spirit.

Simeon is coming, groping his way through thoughts of God and the promised redeemer. And Mary goes to him, smiling, and places the Child in his arms.

His dim eyes brighten. His body stands erect. His purple and scarlet garb no longer drags against his shoulders. His voice bursts into exultant song.

"Now, Master, you can let your servant go in peace!"

He has seen the Son of God, and cannot wait to die. His words bring wonder to the two who gaze and listen.

"A light to enlighten the Gentiles, and the glory of your people, Israel."

Simeon returns the Child into Mary's outstretched arms. He lifts his hands in benediction. He speaks to the Virgin softly.

"You see this child: he is destined for the fall, and for the rising of many in Israel, destined to be a sign that is rejected—and a sword will pierce your own soul too—so that the secret thoughts of many may be laid bare" (Lk 2:25-35).

For a moment Mary wavers. Her hands press Jesus quickly and fearfully closer to her. The blood drains from her face. Her mouth is tortured. But she does not falter. She does not protest. She does not weep.

Joseph, troubled in mind and soul, moves closer to her, knowing by love alone that a blade is quivering in her heart. His eyes are as filled with pain as hers.

Prophecies are racing through her mind:

"He shall be led as a sheep to the slaughter.... For the wickedness of my people have I struck him.... He was wounded for our iniquities, he was bruised for our sins.... They have pierced my hands and my feet. They have numbered all my bones" (Is 53, Ps 22).

All the prophecies since God bade Abraham to sacrifice his son!

On this spot, on this Mount Moriah where the Temple now stands, Abraham built an altar, and bound his son, and took the sword to sacrifice him to the Lord.

Here, perhaps on the very spot where the altar stood, stands our holy Mother, offering the same sacrifice to God. An angel stayed the sword of Abraham, and God provided a ram to be slain and burnt in place of Isaac (Gn 22:1-14).

But no angel shall stay the destiny of Jesus, nor God provide a substitute of any kind for him.

She knows this now. She knows now what it means to be the Mother of God. Yet she stands straight and staunch, a valiant queen, accepting the command of God—and willing it with all her heart.

Getting to Know God

It is the will of God that her Son must die for all of us. Therefore, it is her will as well. The will of God is stronger in her even than her love of Jesus. And more holy.

Only through pain and anguish, borne willingly for the love of God and his holy will, shall she and Jesus—and all of his followers—find any real or lasting joy. Only through crucifixion, impossible as it seems, shall any of us find true bliss. There will be more joy in heaven and earth, and in Mary's own heart, through the death of Jesus, than there was in his birth.

* * *

Now suppose we, each one of us, substitute ourselves for the divine Infant. Inasmuch as Mary is also our mother, we have the privilege—and even the duty—of making this substitution.

Let us think that Mary is presenting us, you and me, to her Father, to her Spouse, and to her Son, our Brother.

What will she say of us on this occasion?

I hate to think what she could say about me, talking to the Trinity as my mother. Suppose she says: "This is a very wicked child; I have been able to do very little with him; I think he should be punished." What then?

Suppose she adds: "But he could be worse, and it might be well to give him another chance." Would I take advantage of that motherly pleading?

I just hope she will be there to present me to God. I wouldn't want to think of facing God alone, without her near me.

Let us think of such a presentation during our lives.

She and Joseph bring us into the temple, the church, up to the altar of sacrifice. And there Simeon, or maybe one of our patron saints, or maybe even a guardian angel, makes some dour prophecy about us.

Suppose this heavenly messenger tells her this child, you or I, is also to be sacrificed—to be blinded, let us say, to be stricken with a long illness, to be put to death unjustly—or anything we can think of for ourselves. What about that?

We do not hear what the messenger tells our Mother. We do not know the fate that awaits us. We do know that Mary will accept it for us. We know she will accept it because it is the will of God, and because if we accept any tragedy, any suffering, it will enrich us beyond all measure.

But will you or I accept it?

That's what matters. It matters to us, and it matters to her.

Will we take it, and how will we take it? Will we cry out that God is unmerciful? Will we even go so far as to say there is no God or he would not, could not, do this to us? Will we whine? Will we ask, "Why should God do this to me?"

Or will we turn to Mary, when the tragedy comes, and say, "It's all right, Mother; God's will be done; but help me to stand the pain?"

Loving God Enough
February 14

The soldier was young, tall, and slender. We saw him at Sunday Mass in the local church. We were going toward the communion rail. He was coming from it. There were ribbons on his uniform that bragged of the medals he had won in battle. He was a handsome kid and evidently a convalescent. This young fellow had seen Death face to face. He had come so close that Death could have kissed him. I was happy it had missed him.

And, just a few moments ago, he had come face to face with Life—eternal Life!

I lifted my eyes from his ribbons to his face. And I saw the shining face of a saint. Catherine and I both stood a moment actually staring at him. His face, I thought, might have been the shining face of Christ. The sun, coming in through the stained glass windows, recalled its splendor. If you saw that face looking at you from the window of some church goods store, you'd say to yourself, "The artist forgot to paint his halo."

I envied him. Desperately I envied him. I wished, moving away from him, that I could love God with half the fervor this boy showed.

I had, sometime before our marriage, decided to be a saint. Come hell or high water, as we Catholics say, I was going to be a saint! I owed that to God. And to Catherine.

And here was a hero home from the wars who made me look like a two-bit mediocre marshmallow holy Joe!

I knew I would never shine that way with the love of God. I would never feel anything like the rapture that kid showed to the world around him. I wasn't his kind. I had no special fervor for God. I didn't like praying on my knees. I never spent more time at the altar than I was supposed to—or was forced to. I felt closer to God out in the country than I did in a cathedral. I had actually fled from some.

How was I going to be a saint if I didn't love God enough? Someone came to my help. St. Martin de Porres maybe, or St. Thérèse of Lisieux, the Little Flower. Perhaps even St. Joseph, or Our Lady herself.

"Nobody loves God enough. Nobody can. So what I want you to do is to love everybody God has made—even the least of Christ's brethren.

"Love your friends. Love your enemies. Love Catherine. Love her apostolate. Love her boys and girls. Love people you don't even like. Love the bores who want to tell you all their woes. Love the people who borrow your money or your books and never return either. Love all the shy and bashful and awkward and lonely and frightened people you touch. And remember that a holy kiss can be a prayer!"

St. Peter himself wrote, "Greet one another with a holy kiss" (1 Pt 5:14).

"The Lord has kissed me with the kiss of his mouth," I thought, as the priest put the Host on my tongue. "And he has given me my new vocation!"

As I walked back to the pew, I recalled a tiny church in a small Italian town, where I saw Franciscan nuns teaching a hundred or more little children to blow kisses to the altar. I was tempted to turn and do as those little children did. But I resisted. Everybody would call me a "show off."

"Every kiss should be a prayer," I thought. "Why can't every prayer become a kiss? Suppose I intend it that way and leave the rest to the Lord! Yes, I must love everybody, and greet some with a holy kiss. I may never become a saint, I thought, but I can sure become a man of prayer!"

Three Cigarettes a Day

A touch of angina pectoris sent me to the Pembroke Hospital late one February night. God had all the northern lights turned on and it was beautiful. "See how he lights up heaven," I said to Catherine as the car sped us to emergency.

Later, I was admitted to the hospital. After a week of many tests, I was handed back my life. Or what was left of it.

"Your aorta is swollen and somewhat sclerosed," the doctor said. "I'll give you some pills for that. In three to six months you'll be as well as ever."

"My aorta!" I exclaimed. "You mean it doesn't work like it orta?"

He pretended he had not heard what I said.

"Go home," he said, "and go to work. But do not work too hard. Do not chop down more than three trees in one day. And do not pick the biggest trees to chop. Everything in moderation. Let that be your motto. Write one book a year. No more. Eat whatever you want. But—for at least six months—no more cigarettes."

Now I had been more of a pipe smoker than a cigarette fiend until they told me about my heart. I took up cigarettes when I began to convalesce.

"You can have three a day," said the doctor in Pembroke one mad March morning, "if that means anything to you."

"You can have ten a day," said another doctor, this one in Combermere, some months later.

Well, that made thirteen cigarettes I could smoke daily. Later the doctor in Chicago told me, "No more." I knew what he meant, of course. No more than thirteen. But I suddenly got superstitious about that number thirteen. So I reversed it. Thirty-one cigarettes a day. That was more like it, I thought. Nobody opposed the idea. But, eventually, I gave up smoking. Abruptly. And completely. (Because the prices went up.)

Praying In Bed

In my hospital room in Pembroke one night I woke to lovely, solemn words route-marching through me. I looked out upon the full, pale glory of the moon, as I inspected the invading words, and wondered about it. It was only making its nightly round to see that the stars were not asleep and that their lamps were clean and glowing. What did I find so wonderful about that? Everything, I realized. Everything was wonderful —because I was alive.

The words that wakened me were wonderful too. They were unfamiliar. I reached for pencil and paper, then looked at their scribbled ranks with awe.

"I am as a stone in your hand, O Lord. Drop me not into the dirty street, nor hurl me from you into the abyss. Keep me close 'til you have need of me!"

The words were a platoon of prayer! Sometimes I pray better in my dreams than in my waking hours. Always I pray better on my back than on my knees.

God is close when one talks to him from a bed. He is a tender Father, stooping low to comfort a sleepy or an ailing child, and easy to talk to then.

He's not a lollypop God or a cop God. He is a Father with a heart full of compassion and a divine sense of humor.

You can anger him, just as you could anger your father. And he might rebuke you, as Christ rebuked Peter. "Get behind me, Satan" (Mk 8:33).

He might punish you, as Jesus whipped the money changers in the Temple; but it would be for your good.

Jesus was, and is, like a father you can talk to. You can't fool him; you can't wheedle him. But you can coax him, if you are sincere. And you can win his complete forgiveness if that is what you really want.

I thought about the strange words I had written. Had I recruited the platoon in a dream? I went back to sleep, but woke to the drum beat of new words:

"Roll me down the mountain sides of the world as a warning, so that sinners may beware of the avalanche of your anger, and may flee to the shelter of your forgiveness.

"Skim me over the water, shallow and deep, to your heart's content, God, so that all the ponds and pools and rivers and seas may become aware of you.

"Tap me against the millions of mystic window panes; so that sleepyheads may be awakened to your love.

"Use me as a weapon against the wolves that eye your flocks.

"I know not what sort of stone I am, granite or quartz or flint or common sandstone, whether I am round and flat, or sharp and jagged. I know only that you, who make all stones, and have pressed rich veins of ore into some, and shining crystals into others, will harden me to your purposes and shape me to your ends. It is good, Lord, to lie, waiting, in your hands."

There was no vein of minerals in me, I knew, nor any crystals. Even if I was just a small gray pebble, I had scratched a sort of letter to almighty God on the granite surface of the years. I've been writing love letters to almighty God ever since.

As a newspaperman I have looked on the writing of these letters as a special assignment. Some reporters cover city hall. Some cover Washington or New York, Europe or the Far East. I cover God! It's the best assignment I've ever had.

He Lived on Eels

After I got out of my sickbed, I ventured to walk to the post office—a whole mile distant from Madonna House! It was a holiday and the place was closed; but I didn't want any mail, I just wanted to see if I could walk that far and come back home the same day.

The wind was blowing a gale; and if I hadn't been so heavy with all the winter stuff I wore I might have been swept into the black waters of the Madawaska River. I loved it. It recalled the night I stood on the bridge of a steamer lost off Cape Hatteras in a storm and tried to shout intelligent words to the captain who permitted me to stay there. I loved that too.

When I did get home I found two missionary priests who had come to visit us. One is a Jesuit, who has a few thousand Native Americans for his flock. The other is a Redemptorist, just back from St. Kitts Island and about to be sent to Japan.

The story of my breath-taking trek through the woods and the wind and the snow—without a dog team—reminded one of them about a young man he had met in the Jesuit seminary.

"This chap came in grumbling about something that had been served for dinner that evening. He was also grumbling about one or two of the seminary rules. He made an extremely bad impression on me. In my vanity, I thought to myself that he was much too lightweight for the priesthood. Then, in my arrogance, I decided to question him and show him up to himself.

"He said he had met the Jesuits in Australia and decided to become one of them. He was sent to Ireland, and while he was studying there he met a missionary who was asking for volunteers for Alaska. He said he believed it was the will of God, so he volunteered.

"'And do you think you can stand it?' I asked.

"'Father,' he answered with great passion, 'I hate Alaska. I was afraid of it all the time I was there, its vastness, its tremendous silence, its intolerable loneliness. But I talked to another Jesuit who has been there for twenty years. He said he is still afraid, so I felt better.'

"It was shocking to think he had been there, and left. But, thank God, I didn't leave the subject alone. I began to ask him questions about Alaska. I wanted to know, especially, why he hated it.

"'Well,' he said, 'one reason is there was little food, at least where I was. I had to live on eels all one winter and nothing else. You put nails in a long pole, break a hole in the ice, thrust in your pole, turn it with both hands, keep turning it, and eventually you get your eels.'

"I began to see why a man like this should be permitted to grumble a little at what was served him for dinner—just as an old soldier can be readily excused for grousing and griping at the army. I began to feel ashamed of my feelings for this chap; but I was still of the opinion that he was a lightweight.

"Eventually I asked him about dog teams, and he told me as dramatic an incident as I remember. He had gone about three hundred miles with fourteen dogs and a sled full of supplies. He had delivered the supplies and he was mushing home early the next morning.

"'I hadn't gone far,' he said, 'when I happened to see a gray half-moon break out of the woods back of me and to my right. Wolves! About two or three hundred of them! I strapped myself to the sled, got my rifle out, got my cartridges ready, and then stopped the dog team.'

"'You stopped the dog team?' I couldn't help saying. 'In the name of heaven, why?'

"'Well,' he explained, 'you know when you stop the team, the dogs always look around. They looked around. They saw the wolves. And they were off down the road in a streak. I didn't have to say a word to them.

"'I got about twenty wolves, which delayed the pack some; but we didn't stop until the dogs were too weary to run another inch. That was about thirty hours after we had sighted the wolf pack.

"'I put my little tent around the bole of a big tree, spread the dogs in a circle outside the tent, and made camp for the night. If the wolves were still following us, the dogs would know and would wake me with their barking. And if the wolves came too close and I couldn't get away, I could climb the tree.'

"'But man,' I objected, 'that was madness. You would have frozen to death there.'

"'No,' he said. 'I might have got frostbitten, of course. But some of those dogs were sure to get home. Then a rescue party would set out. I would be found. One of our fellows was treed for two days, in just such circumstances. And he's still alive.'

"'Young man,' I said, 'I don't blame you a bit for leaving Alaska.'

"'Oh,' he answered, 'I only left long enough to finish up my studies. I will be ordained next month. Then I am going back to Alaska, and I'll stay there, I guess, until I die or go crazy. You see, I'm sure that's where God wants me to work.'"

The priest was silent for a moment or two, thinking.

"I was so ashamed of myself, judging this man for grumbling over a dish of beans improperly cooked," he said then, "that I've never got over it. And I've tried never to judge anyone since then."

———

Freeing the Man Possessed

In the Gospel of Mark, we see where Jesus freed a man of legions of devils who were besieging him, making him mad; he sent them into swine (Mk 5:1-20).

I think people possessed are like swine. Pigs are greedy, pushing everybody away from the trough. They're ambitious, rude, most selfish, even eating their own little piglets sometimes. Maybe that's something of what the story means.

But to me, the whole meaning of the story boils down to the reaction of the people. They were scandalized that Jesus should destroy these pigs which were a livelihood for so many.

My guess is that these people were dealing, in a black-market sort of way, with the Jews, feeding them pork, which was forbidden. And Jesus, taking it into his own hands, got rid of both levels of pork in one single gesture!

"There go all your pork chops thundering down the hill. Look at 'em diving into the lake!" I'm not sure, but I think Jesus had a good laugh watching that thundering herd of hogs rush down the hillside into the sea. He sent demons from the man into the clean sea, to be buried forever and ever.

That is what happens to our sins when they come out of us in confession. They dash frantically down, down, down, down, into the depths of utter forgetfulness, never to be remembered any more by God, and hopefully not by us either.

There's something in this story that Jesus is trying to tell us. It has to do with our sins, with their being utterly drowned. Once we have confessed them, once we have felt sorry for them, Jesus has swept them away into the waters of forgetfulness.

And it doesn't matter what people say about us—"What a nice guy he used to be before he got religion!" Nothing matters except that now we are free of devils, free of sin. And God loves us very much, and we are in a position to love him back.

March

Maker of Puzzles

Dear God, Father of Us All,

When I saw those jigsaw puzzles, it did not occur to me that you had sent them as spiritual reading. They were temptations and distractions. I succumb easily to temptations and distractions. And challenges have always lured me—to happiness or woe.

There was plenty of work calling to me; but I pretended not to hear it, and I sat for hours over those queer jigsaw bits, selecting them one at a time in order to make a beautiful mosaic. Selecting and rejecting. This fits here. It fits perfectly. But the colors are wrong. Obviously it does not belong here, whether it fits or not. Ah, here is the piece I want! No! It is the right color but it does not fit. It almost fits. But it is just as wrong as if it had an entirely different color.

Keep looking. Keep searching. (This is me, Lord, talking to myself.) There is only one piece in that pile of seven hundred, or a thousand, or a thousand and some. One special piece that fits here, and no place else. Rub your eyes. Wipe your glasses. Get a magnifying glass. Look through all the blue pieces. What you want has to be blue. It has to be a particular shade of blue. And it has to have a thin white line on one end of it—a white line as thin as a hair. Keep looking. Keep searching. You'll find it eventually. The needle in the haystack? Easy—if you had a magnet. The magnet here is patience—but a good eye wouldn't hurt.

Lord, I began to doubt. Suppose the piece I wanted was not there! This was a donation, this puzzle. Other people had sat over it, enjoying it. They had broken it up, afterward. And they had sent it that others might enjoy it. Perhaps someone had been careless when he put the pieces back in the box. Maybe some pieces fell, were swept up and burnt.

I likened the puzzle to the clothes I wear, the things I eat, the things given me for my use. There was love in the sending of these things; and there is love in accepting them—love for the donors, love for you. It was in keeping with our way of life in this apostolate that there should be pieces missing. Yet even with pieces missing, the puzzles fascinated me.

Sometimes, in their leisure moments, the girls came in to help me. Sometimes they sat and talked to me.

"Why does God love me?" one asked. "I am nobody, just an ordinary girl. There is not a thing special about me. Absolutely nothing! There isn't a single thing about me anybody could love. I know God loves me, but why should he?"

Even while I contemplate a jigsaw puzzle, Lord, you are with me, talking to me, talking through me to others.

"Do you love him?" I asked.

"Of course." Her tone implied that my question was silly, because everybody loved God, even ordinary people.

"God loves the baby just born," I said, "though it is neither good nor bad."

"Oh." The girl tossed that argument aside, and picked up a piece I had been looking for, one that had eluded me for hours. She dropped it into place with no feeling of accomplishment. It was as if she had seen a place that needed sweeping and had swept it. "Oh, of course God loves a baby. A baby cannot sin."

"Neither can it practice virtue," I said. "God loves every creature he has made. He loves the good, the indifferent, and the bad. He loves those who sin against him. He sent his Son to earth to be a man, to die, to redeem all sinners—especially the worst of them. If he loves sinners who do not love him, who may even hate him, how much more does he love those who love him? Especially those like you, who give their whole lives to him?"

"Thanks," the girl said. "I love him. But I am such a drip, such a mess! I am glad to realize he loves me. I guess a girl has to be told, every so often, that someone loves her. Imagine though, being lucky enough to be loved by God!"

The jigsaw puzzle became, Lord, not just a temptation or a snare after that. It did indeed become spiritual reading, a book of meditations.

Every creature of yours is as complicated as any such puzzle. We little bits of flesh and bone and color and odd shapes—we are all jigsaw pieces. Some of us are where you want us; where you planned, through all eternity, that we should be. Having a free will, though, we can ignore you, God, and go where we don't belong. We can even fall off your table and be thrown out with the trash.

We do not see the mosaic into which we have been destined to fit. We will see it only when you reveal it to us.

You fit us all together; the living and the dead and the generations not yet born. You play with us continually. You love each piece, the drab as well as the bright; the outside pieces distinguished by their straight edges, as well as the crazy-shaped bits that are interlocked somewhere in the middle.

You too must find there are some pieces missing—against your will. I wonder if you do not feel more sorrow over that than anyone on earth can realize.

Thank you for the puzzles, Lord. Thanks for placing me where I belong. If you find that I've grown out of the shape you gave me—that I've become warped or bloated—or that the color you gave me has faded, through my own fault, and no longer entitles me to this particular place—then, God, remove me!

But do not let me fall off your table. Do not let me be swept away from you. Do not permit me to be cast into the fire!

Because, like that girl, I too love you, God.

Your not-irreplaceable jig

Persecutions
St. Patrick's Day
March 17

Are you afraid? Many people are afraid of being ridiculed for the sake of Christ or God. Many people are afraid of what people will say if they go to church, or stand up for what they believe.

We're not persecuted today as Christians were in St. Paul's day. He had his head cut off and St. Peter was crucified upside-down. All the apostles except St. John were martyrs. It was a tough thing in those days to be a man of God.

And it's a tough thing today, too, sometimes to be a man of God or a woman of God. You're looked upon with suspicion. "What does she see in religion? What does it get her? Surely there's some catch to it.

"What's the gimmick? What satisfaction does she get out of it, following Christ like that? The only satisfaction she gets is a crown of thorns and a splinter or two of the cross every once in a while."

But persevere in following Christ, and you will receive your reward. You will get your place in heaven. It'll be a great place, and a great day for all of us—even a greater day than St. Patrick's Day!

Humility
St. Joseph, Husband of Mary
March 19

Always, always, always, Jesus preaches humility: be humble, be hidden, be little, hide yourself, give first place to others. Remember that part of the Gospel where he placed a little child in the midst of the crowd and declared that if anyone wants to become great, he must become like the little child (Mt 18:3).

So if we want to become great in the eyes of the Lord, we must not seem to be great in the eyes of others. We must not strive for official positions or great places in the world. We do the best we can with what we have, with what talents the Lord has given us. And that's all.

Especially we don't want any fame; we don't want any attention. If we get it, we take it, but we don't strive for it. It's strange, very strange, but the more you fly from greatness, the more people seek you out and make you think that you are great! But no man is great except by the grace of God, and only by the grace of God.

A "great man," according to the world's standards, could be corrupt, vicious, even insane. But a great man in the eyes of God would be a man like Joseph, the spouse of Mary, who never tried to get into the limelight and who even now is so obscure that you hardly ever hear sermons about him. Yet, he was the one chosen to be the patron of the universal Church!

It's hard to be humble. We feel slighted if we're not recognized or if we're not in the highest place. Our feelings are hurt. Inside we say, "What the hell, I'll show them who I am!"

But the Holy Spirit makes us love these slights to our "importance." Then we think, "Well, maybe I'm not as big as I thought I was." It's good for us to think like that, because it's the truth.

By living in the truth, we grow in real greatness, and all our opinions about greatness are changed by the Spirit of God. He teaches us what it is to be truly great in the eyes of God.

The Woman at the Well

> When Jesus heard that the Pharisees had found out that he was making ... more disciples than John ... he left Judaea and went back to Galilee. This meant that he had to cross Samaria. (See Jn 4:1-42)

A divine impatience was calling Jesus to take his disciples and go further north. He could not resist its urging.

It was a woman who summoned him. A beautiful, seductive, intelligent woman. She was a restless, world-worn, love-hungry, disillusioned idealist. She had no religion. She knew nothing of theology and ritual and respectability. She made no show of virtue. She did not fast, nor did she pray in public. The law of Moses never wooed or worried her. She was not timid; she was bold. She was a sinner, and she acknowledged it. And she could be a saint, for she contained much love!

She was a soul worth walking miles for; and Jesus walked those miles so rapidly his disciples had trouble keeping up with him. When he reached his goal, the shade of the trees near Jacob's well, it was noon. He sent his friends into the nearby town of Sichar, so they could buy provisions—and so he could be alone with the woman.

She had a rendezvous with God, but didn't know it. She came to the well at this hour because there would be no little snips of girls looking at her in that silly way they had; nor any of their elders who thought themselves so righteous and so pure. She could do without them. She could do without all other women. And without men too, if anyone should ask her. To her, one man was as vicious and stupid and hopeless as another. They were clods. And love was a stranger to them.

She had once believed that someday she would find a man worth a woman's love, a man worth working for, worth suffering for, worth fighting for, worth dying for. But now she was sure there was no such man. Now she believed love was a blossom without roots. It withered and died in a night. It had to be thrown away, like a weed.

She saw the Man waiting at the well, and came toward him with provoking slowness, unconsciously moving her shapely hips. He was a Jew. But magnificent! And there was an air of distinction about him. And a sense of tremendous power. He was watching her. She felt ridiculous. What could such a man want of her?

He wanted a drink of water! She was surprised only because he had spoken to her and had asked a favor. Men did not talk to women in any public place. And a Jew did not talk to a Samaritan, especially a Samaritan woman. The Jews regarded the Samaritans as heretics and schismatics; and the Samaritans hated and feared the Jews.

This Man was apparently above all these petty and hateful rules and regulations. He made his own rules! She began to feel at ease. She asked a few questions; and shivered delightedly as she saw his eyes catch fire. What a breathtaking Man he was!

He surprised her further by saying that if she knew who it was that asked her for a drink, perhaps she would have asked the gift of him, and he would have given her living water.

Somehow she knew what he meant by living water. He meant love such as she had dreamed of in wretched moments. There was something like love even now in his eyes. She could not be mistaken. She knew love when she saw it. But this was a different kind of love, one she had never known. This was a love that could not be sullied or spoiled in any way, that never could be less than what it was; that had only begun to grow!

Yet even as she savored the truth, she denied it. There was no use fooling herself. It would only make life harder. The Man was speaking of the living water in the well. Jacob's well. It was a thousand years old, or more, so far as she knew; yet it was still alive. Jacob had provided it. Was the Stranger greater than Jacob? Did he have water with more life in it?

"Whosoever drinks of this water will thirst again," Jesus said. "But he who drinks of the water I give him, shall not thirst for ever. The water shall become a fountain in him, springing up into life everlasting."

She had been right at first. He did mean love, everlasting love.

"Sir," she begged, "give me this water that I may not thirst, nor come here again to draw water from this well." If she could have love, and never go back to any man again ...!

"Go call your husband," Jesus said. "and come back with him."

"I have no husband," she said. She felt trapped. And she felt shamed. She had been given a taste of heaven, and it had been snatched away from her by the Man who showed it to her. Because she was not worthy of it!

"You have answered well," Jesus said, "telling me you have no husband. You have had five; and the man you live with now is not your husband." She looked at him closely. He was not condemning her! His eyes told her he understood, sympathized, pitied, forgave. He was a prophet! How did a woman talk to a prophet? What did one say to him? Something about worshipping God, perhaps, "Our fathers adored God on this mountain," she said, "and you say he should be adored only in Jerusalem." Why did he not blast her? How was it that she could stand in the presence of such a Man—feeling the vilest of sinners, yet not wanting to be anywhere else in the world?

"Woman," Jesus said—she took new heart at the way he said that word—"the time will come when God will be adored neither in Jerusalem nor there on Mount Gerazim. You adore that which you know not; we adore that which we know, for salvation is of the Jews. The hour approaches when the faithful will adore in spirit and in truth. God is a Spirit, and they who adore him must adore in spirit and in truth."

She waited, loving the music of his voice, the wonder of his words. But he seemed to have said all he had to say. That must not be! She must hold him a little longer. Perhaps if she talked about the Messiah, he might stay a little longer. "When the Messiah comes," she ventured, "he will tell us everything we need to know."

"I am he," Jesus said, revealing his secret for the first time. "I who am speaking to you, am the Messiah."

She knew he spoke the truth. She knew it by his eyes, and by the fountain of living water that had sprung up within her. She had been miraculously cleansed in body and soul; and she would have flung herself at the Savior's feet in love and gratitude and adoration, had not the disciples come into sight, burdened with the food they had bought in Sichar. She hurried away, leaving her waterpot behind her. The noon heat was pitiless, but she ran as though there were no burning sun above her, and as though she were a little girl. She was going to tell all her friends she had met the Messiah, the Christ, who had told her all about herself. She had gone to confession to him, and he had not scolded her at all. He had washed her in the living water of his love. She would be clean forevermore, and forevermore she would be happy. "Come and see the Christ!" she cried again and again. "Come and see the Christ!"

Philip and Bartholomew pretended not to have seen anything amiss. They approached Jesus solemnly, holding out food to him. But he was not hungry. He refused their offerings. "I have meat to eat which you know not," he said. "My meat is to do the will of him who sent me, that I may perfect his work."

He knelt in prayer, thanking his Father for the soul he had gained. The sinful Samaritan had become a new lay apostle of his kingdom; and she would bring him others.

Philip and Bartholomew squatted in the dust, wishing Jesus had chosen a spot in the shade, wishing the place weren't so silent, so dead. They munched their food as quietly as they could, until Philip stirred and shot upright, knowing a queer sort of fear. "Look, Master," he said. "People rushing toward us!"

Jesus rose, smiling. "Do you not say there are four months between sowing and reaping?" he asked. "Lo, a few moments ago I planted one small seed. Now, behold, lift up your eyes and see! The fields are already white, and ready for harvest. One man sows. Another reaps. The fruit is gathered into life everlasting. And both sower and reaper may rejoice together. I send you to reap what you did not sow, and to harvest the fruit of the Sower's toil."

Here, at Jacob's well, far from Jerusalem, countless Samaritans declared that Jesus was indeed "the Savior of the world."

Cleansing the Temple

> Jesus went up to Jerusalem, and in the Temple he found people selling cattle and sheep and pigeons, and the money changers sitting at their counters there.
>
> (See Jn 2:13-22)

Nobody knew Jesus when he entered the Temple with Philip and Bartholomew; but they saw he was someone of great importance and authority, for his eyes blazed with such anger that men shivered and sought to escape his gaze.

He was angry at what he saw in the Court of the Gentiles, and with what he heard.

The holy place reeked with the smell of cattle and sheep and goats and doves waiting to be sold and slaughtered. The beautiful floor was littered with the droppings of sheep and the dung of oxen. The air was filled with fat buzzing flies; and the floor was crawling with vermin. Men selling and buying animals for sacrifice haggled and cursed and quarrelled. The animals, even the most patient of them, made sad noises, calling to their mothers—or to their lambs and calves. Money changers, arrogant and greedy, counted coins in loud and blaspheming voices—and cheated as many as they could.

This in the house built to honor his Father, the most beautiful and ornate building in the world! Gold and marble everywhere—and everywhere filth and stench and avarice and lies!

All over Galilee, among the poorest of the poor, God was worshipped piously. Here, where holiness was to be expected, among the richest of the rich, among the priests and Levites and doctors of the law, people worshipped mammon and robbed the hundreds of thousands of pilgrims who had come to honor God.

Pieces of rope lay on the dirty floor. Wherever beasts are brought to market there are ropes. Jesus picked up a few lengths and made a scourge of them. Holding this in his right hand, he flung himself into an attack on those who had defiled the Temple, lashing right and left. Yet in spite of his holy wrath, he took care—it seemed to Lucifer, who was watching—not to inflict any serious bodily injuries. He showed the fury of an avenging angel together with the concern of a human father. He wanted those sinners to recognize the enormity of their sin, and to be sorry for it, even while he punished them! Was it possible he loved those thieves and cheaters? Lucifer noted that Jesus did not lay a rope's end on any of the sellers of doves. He did not speak harshly to them. He bade them take the birds out of the Temple, and to keep them out. Nothing more than that.

The dealers, some of them powerful brutes and noted brawlers, ran in panic, slipping and sliding in the piles of dung, rising, falling, scrambling toward the gates, frightening the sheep and oxen so that they stampeded, bleating and bellowing, and rushed everywhere, colliding with one another, leaping over one another, fighting for freedom. The air was filled with a thousand frantic wings; and the floor was filled with thousands of spinning, circling, jingling, wheeling coins—and with scores of ragged little boys.

"My Father's house," Jesus shouted at the fleeing horde, "was meant to be a house of prayer. You have made it a den of thieves."

Lucifer was watching. He began to doubt Jesus was God. Jesus had been fearsome in his anger, but he had not been Godlike. When the Most High was provoked, he did not make a mere scourge of ropes. He poured down fire and brimstone from flaming skies. He burned whole cities. He buried people alive. If Jesus were the true Son of such a Father, how could he be so mild?

Maybe he meant what he had said about his Father's love for humanity, his Father's justice, and his Father's mercy. Maybe he was influencing his Father to temper justice with mercy—even to be more merciful than just! If the Most High were to listen to this Man, Lucifer thought, and to spread his divine mercy as a carpet for people to walk on with their dirty feet, it would mark the beginning of the end of the kingdom of hell on earth.

Lucifer would be helpless—unless he could induce them to reject God's mercy, to despise it, or to have no faith in it.

After a little while, the chief priests came, the Pharisees, the Scribes, the doctors of the law, and the Sadducees. Unsmiling men who wanted an explanation from the Man with the scourge of ropes. They could not accuse him of any crime, for they knew the cattle and sheep should not have been permitted in the Temple, nor the dealers in animals and coins. Each one of them, Lucifer saw clearly, felt guilty—too guilty to look at Jesus squarely. They squinted red eyes at him. They made gestures to show their feelings.

But all they dared say was to ask by what authority he had acted.

Jesus looked at them sorrowfully. But his speech was almost gay.

"Destroy this Temple," he said, "and in three days I will raise it up."

That, he knew, would sound like a riddle to them or like sheer foolishness. He was speaking of his body; the real Temple of the Lord. He was thinking of his crucifixion, and of his resurrection on the third day.

Now they looked at him. And now they gave vent to the anger that churned in them. It had taken forty-six years to build this Temple, they told him. And he would rise it up in three days if it were destroyed? Bah!

The devil was as pleased as a demon could be; for now the masters of Israel were on his side. It was they who profited most from the sale of animals and doves. They bought the beasts cheap and sold them for ungodly sums. They also had an interest in the money changers' profits. Businessmen such as they did not scruple to take drastic measures when their business was endangered.

They were good at offering sacrifices, these priests. Let them sacrifice the Christ then—if, indeed, he was the Christ!

Only one thing puzzled the devil.

Lucifer was sure that Jesus referred to himself when he spoke of the Temple, but the matter of three days baffled him. If Jesus meant he would come back from the dead three days after Lucifer had destroyed him, he was wrong. Nobody ever came back from the tomb through his own power.

April

Easter Parade

It is Holy Saturday. People in the cities are getting ready for Easter. There will be a great parade on Fifth Avenue tomorrow, one on Powell Street, another on Michigan Avenue, and one at Sunset Boulevard and Vine Street. And in Harlem. The Harlem parade will be the most colorful, the most gorgeous, the most amazing.

I shall not see these parades. I would not take part in one, even if I were able to. Nor do I long to be a spectator.

While I have rested here by the window, I have seen a different kind of Easter Parade, a parade of the days. I have seen them bring in the spring. I have seen them make the world ready for the day of glory. I have seen them set the stage for the spectacle of the Resurrection.

Of Easter and Liturgists

The train is bumping eastward. It is difficult to write. I could work more easily on the inside of a cocktail shaker, if I could crawl into one. But who cares? I am hurrying home for Easter. The special Mass. The special foods! The kiss of peace—that three-in-one salute we give each other on the cheeks with the greeting "Christ is risen!" and with the answer, "Truly, he is risen." The knocking together of gaily colored eggs. The special Easter bread and rich spread. And that spine-tingling Easter Proclamation, that incomparable hymn of exultation—the *Exsultet*. Above all, Lord, I am thinking of the Exsultet! My memory of Father Callahan singing the Exsultet redeems the sins of this foul roadbed!

Lord, have I become a liturgist? I used to be allergic to anything liturgic. Was it my natural lethargy, my natural stupidity, or my natural orneriness? It seemed to me that the average liturgist was as strident and strutting about rules and regulations for divine worship as the old Pharisees, or as some modern editors were about the writing of news. Some of these, Lord, insisted that no story should begin with the article "the." I rebelled. I broke every writing rule I could—and usually got away with it. I reacted to the liturgy lads the same way. When one told me it was improper to say the Rosary during Mass, I felt rebuked. And I felt like rebuking back.

"Not improper," I said. "You mean impossible. What with the priest whispering parts of the Mass, and saying some out loud, and singing other parts sometimes, a guy gets distracted. And there are the altar boys ringing bells like they were paid for it, and falling over their clumsy little feet, carrying books and stuff. And sometimes a choir's singing, on or off key. Sure it's impossible."

I guess I was always a brash and callow fool. There was certainly nothing of this "rapture stuff" in all my speckled soul. You know I still can't say a single Hail Mary without distractions. You know, Lord, how I feel when I read the extravagant words of some of the saints....

"Our dear eternity ... our most sweet consolation and reward ... most dear St. Joseph ... most sweet St. Theresa."

My vaulting vertigo!

I don't believe I could ever make baby talk to you, God, even if I should become a fervent saint. I am no mystic, though I do seem to hear your voice now and then—though never with my ears. Yet there have been times when my emotions have rocked the chapel.

When Cardinal Rugambwa, while he was still a bishop, visited us at Madonna House one Holy Thursday and sang the Our Father, I felt a glad earthquake in me. For the first time in all my years, I realized the meaning of "Our Father."

It was your Son, Jesus, in that delightful African bishop, who addressed you as "Our Father." His Father and mine! Ours! Father of all the people in the world, black, white, yellow, red, brown and all the various mixtures of those colors. How could I help shaking, realizing in that flash of light that all of us were so closely related to each other, and to you?

We felt blessed and honored. We took that tall, black, handsome man, that humble smiling Christ, to the deepest parts of our hearts. We sang songs to him that first night at dinner. We had a royal feast and a riot of music. We felt as though you yourself had come to dine with us.

I was unusually elated, but in my usual, fumbling, humpty-dumpty, happy-go-daffy way, I pretended to take everything in my stride. But with the Exsultet, I gave in. I gave in all the way. I even gave in to myself!

You tried in many ways to teach me something about the liturgy; but I refused to learn. You did everything a long-suffering God could do. You failed. But at last you had your way with me! God bless you, God—if I may put it that way.

I was in the chapel shortly after eleven o'clock on Holy Saturday evening. I watched the priest kindle the fire. I saw the incense begin to burn. I saw the paschal candle lighted.

Then the electric light snapped off, and the candle, symbolizing Christ, the Light of the World, was slowly carried down the center aisle.

"Light of Christ!" our chaplain, Father Callahan, sang. "Thanks be to God!" we answered.

Twice more he sang as he came toward the altar; and many candles, lit from the paschal flame, were being held erect. The light of Christ was burning in many places in the world.

Before I quite realized what was happening, Father Callahan began to sing the Exsultet. It was then your tide of grace seeped into me, flooding me.

There was a book in my hand, which someone had carelessly left near me. And there was light enough to read.

> Rejoice, heavenly powers! Sing, choirs of angels!
> Exult, all creation around God's throne!
> Jesus Christ, our King, is risen!
> Sound the trumpet of salvation!
>
> Rejoice, O earth, in shining splendor,
> radiant in the brightness of your King!
> Christ has conquered! Glory fills you!
> Darkness vanishes for ever!
>
> Rejoice, O Mother Church! Exult in glory!
> The risen Savior shines upon you!
> Let this place resound with joy,
> echoing the mighty song of all God's people!

I was helpless against the deluge, helpless and dazed. I caught at the words as they went by, and clung to them as though they were as precious as life itself.

> My dearest friends, standing with me in this holy light ...,
>
> This is our Passover feast,
> when Christ, the true Lamb, is slain,
> whose blood consecrates the homes of all believers.
>
> This is the night when first you saved our fathers:
> you freed the people of Israel from their slavery
> and led them dry-shod through the sea....
>
> Father, how wonderful your care for us!
> How boundless your merciful love!
> To ransom a slave
> you gave away your Son.

There was more beauty in those words than I had glimpsed in shell or flower or star or bird or stone or stream or forest. And I was walking dry-shod through a red sea of my own, bringing those words with me.

> Most blessed of all nights, chosen by God
> to see Christ rising from the dead!
>
> Night truly blessed when heaven is wedded to earth
> and man is reconciled with God!
> (Easter Proclamation, Easter Vigil)

At last I realized that the liturgy was more than rubrics, more than rules and regulations and rituals. And I knew, eventually, that you were talking to me, God. That is, your ideas were rattling around in all that empty space I call my mind; and you were bringing them, slowly, into a disciplined and orderly array of words.

"The liturgy is not in the beautiful and profound words alone. Nor in the words or gestures of the priest. Nor in his voice. Nor in the voices of the exalted boys and girls around you. Look at them. They are even happier than you. It is not in the ornaments on the altar, nor in the burning of wax tapers, not in the smell of the incense, not in the ritual set down in official books. But it is in all these things together.

"Through all the beauty it can gather up—beauty of words, of tone, of music, of rich aroma, of gold and silver vessels, of brocaded vestments, of symbols and ceremonies and gestures, the Church, the bride of my Son, woos her Beloved. And officially she says, 'This is the way best to show him our love, to woo him; let us be one in him as he is one in us.'

"This is the liturgy. I have given it to you. I have spread beauty before all your senses that you may fill yourself with it and offer it to me. I have blessed your eyes, your ears, your nostrils, your mind, your heart, your hands, your feet, your mouth. I have blessed you all, that you may all bless me.

"This is the liturgy. I am the creator of the liturgy. I am I. I am God. Out of my mouth comes the Word. The Word I utter is I. I am the Father of the Word. I am the Word. I am the voice that utters the Word. I am the Concord, the Love, that exists between the Voice and the Word. I am the Father, the Son, and the Holy Spirit. I am the Three in One, the One in Three. I am the Crucified. I am the Resurrection and the Life. I am the Eternal Kiss that you will feel before the Mass is done."

If I wasn't exactly dead, I was living in a tomb of ignorance, with a great stone of orneriness rolled against the door. Your flood has washed me out of the tomb. You are my Resurrection and my Life.

A happy Easter, God, from your addled Easter egg.

A Prayer of Joy

The ducks have returned to the Madawaska River. They are pretending to be jet planes, dive bombers, torpedoes, or snorkel submarines. I wish I could enjoy the icy water as they do.

The pussy willows have grown so big I could mistake them, at a distance, for choke cherry buds. The maple tree near the river has acquired a million little buttons. Pike and bass are spawning in the slough; and someone has set a trap for muskrats.

A late snow falls. Great white flakes. And someone nearby has made a bonfire of last year's fallen twigs and branches. I love the smell of wood smoke. Lord, let it come up to you as incense for your new April. And let me offer with it a prayer of perfect joy!

There are people offering their pain to you as prayer. There are people offering prayers in atonement for misdeeds or grievous sins. There are people offering prayers of supplication, and prayers of petition, and prayers of faith and love and hope. But prayers of joy, I think, are very few. Yet we have most need of you when we are most happy.

What do we need to make us happy? A new convertible with red leather seats? A final payment on the first mortgage? A boy friend? A well-paying job, or a promotion with twice as much money? A new suit or hat? A broiled lobster and half a keg of beer? A trip to Europe or some other expensive continent?

Once I worked for most of these things—and only for them. Now my happiness is made of little things. The sun rising in the blazing east. A marigold in full bloom. A sparrow staring at me from a post. A mushroom ready to pick. A hamburger or hot dog, with French mustard, or perhaps a dash of horse-radish, or even a plate of spinach with melted cheese. A bunch of wild flowers brought into my room. Sunset and evening star. The faces of happy friends.

* * *

My heart is still full of the joy it found in the blue agates I once found on a little Texas mountain. "You love blue, God," I said, "because it is Our Lady's color. You use it constantly and you delight to use it. Blue bells. Bluebirds. Blue stars. Blue skies. Blue stones. My Catherine's blue eyes. You make a man glad that he can see."

Climbing that little Texas mountain, Lord, was like walking through the main aisle of a jewelry store, with your gifts lying carelessly everywhere—on the rocks, in the crevices, and in the ants' nests beneath the all-embracing thorn bushes and the spines of cactus plants. There was not a single salesman in your store to bully or harass me, no other customer to snatch a bargain from me, nobody checking a price, nobody figuring out the tax, nobody limiting my selections, nobody who might suspect I was a shoplifter or some other sort of crook.

My pockets were half-filled before I reached the top. I glanced down the slope between me and the road; and I seemed to be looking at the pathway of my years. How rusty and barren it was! How covered with grit and dust! How tangled with briars and barbs and poisonous thorns! And perhaps there were nests of rattlesnakes hiding there, coiled on warm rocks or hidden beneath the greasewood.

I felt like a wayward child. And you bade me be a child. "A child has implicit trust in his father," you said. "A child is simple. A child loves, and seeks love. A child tries to know the will of his father and to act according to that will. A child has faith. A child has hope. A child has a great humility. A child is pure in heart and mind. A child has wisdom too—sometimes more wisdom than any of his elders. And unless you are a child, you shall not inherit the kingdom of heaven."

I started down the little mountain leisurely, carefully, thinking of your words, thinking of your Son who also loved to walk upon your maintains.

I pondered the sermon on the mount (Mt 5-7). Christ must have talked from a mountain such as this. Not too high. Not too steep. Not too far from the highways, the routes of caravans. I wondered a little about his temptation in the desert, where the devil suggested Jesus should transform the stones to bread (Mt 4:1-4). Did the imp have any idea, then, that someday your Son would transform bread into his Body, and feed a hungry world?

As I moseyed further down the slope, I was almost blinded by the brilliance of your acres of quartz and calcite crystals lying in the sun. They sparkled with splinters of your glory.

The Transfiguration of your Son happened on a mountain. "And his face shone as the sun, and his garments became white as snow." And you cried out, from behind a bright cloud, "This is my beloved Son, in whom I am well pleased: hear ye him" (Mt 17:1-5).

The stones of my little mountainside were transfigured. They shone like little suns. They were white as snow. I fell upon them like a greedy gamin, stuffing my pockets until they bulged. I kissed some of them, dust and all, because you were pleased with them, because they told me so delightfully of your love.

Lord, if you come hunting human stones, please bring Our Lady with you. Let her raise me in her blessed fingers and touch me to her holy lips before she shows me to you! Then I shall be transfigured! I shall shine with borrowed glory. And you will be pleased with me, your happy pebble.

I ask this mercy in the name of your Son, Jesus, for myself and all the other dull stones in the world. Lord, give us luster, through Our Lady, that we may show your love—and your joy—to all the stony world.

Fish and Taxes

April 15

When they came to Capernaum, the collectors of the half-shekel tax went up to Peter and said, "Does not your teacher pay the tax?" He said, "Yes." And when he came home, Jesus spoke to him first, saying, "What do you think, Simon? From whom do kings of the earth take toll or tribute? From their sons or from others?" And when he said, "From others," Jesus said to him, "Then the sons are free. However, not to give offense to them, go to the sea and cast a hook, and take the first fish that comes up, and when you open its mouth you will find a shekel; take that and give it to them for me and for yourself."

(Mt 17:24-27)

Simon Peter looked upon Jesus as the holiest of holy prophets, whom a sinner must approach in fear and trembling. Jesus, who had come to rescue sinners, and who had an abiding love for them, was not entirely pleased with Peter's attitude.

He wanted Peter to love him perfectly, and perfect love casts out fear. To bring the fisherman closer to him, he arranged a private miracle for him; one that was as divinely amusing as it was baffling.

They were in Capernaum. One of the men who collected the Temple taxes had looked with something of a sneer at Peter, and asked if his master did not intend to pay the tax. Peter's impulse was to strike the man for such blasphemous impudence. No man should sneer when he spoke of Jesus. But he controlled himself.

"Of course," he said. He merely scowled at the man, and hurried to find Jesus and ask what he should do. He felt somewhat guilty. How had he dared answer for Jesus, when he had no idea of Jesus' feeling about the tax?

Jesus met Peter with a strange and mysterious smile. And he asked a question that Peter mistook for a riddle.

"From whom do the kings of earth demand tolls or tribute? From their sons or from others?"

"From others," Peter said.

"Then the sons are exempt," Jesus remarked.

Abruptly Peter knew what the Lord was talking about. He was saying that he and Peter were sons of God, and therefore not obliged to pay the Temple tax! He had bracketed himself with Peter, the wretched sinner! Such love as he had never known before took hold of Peter's heart and squeezed it.

"But," Jesus added—and now there was a gleam in his eyes that made Peter think of a mischievous boy planning a silly prank to play on one of his too-solemn professors—"lest we scandalize some people, let us pay the tax."

It was astonishing to think of Jesus, the Messiah, as a man with a sense of humor. Yet that's what he was—at least at the moment. Peter waited impatiently for the words of explanation he expected. But Jesus did not explain. Not exactly.

"Go to the sea," he said. "Cast a hook, and take the fish that comes up."

"One fish?"

Peter forgot this was some sort of joke. It wasn't possible to sell a fish, even a big one, for the money needed. Maybe the Rabbi didn't mean to sell the fish, though. What then? Was he going to have it cooked for the tax collector—and serve it as a sort of gift? No. He most certainly was not. Jesus never bribed anybody, even his disciples. He told them what to do, and they did it. Peter felt as he had the day Jesus told him to strike out for the deep and cast the nets (Lk 5:4-7). It might be a silly order; but it was an order. He would obey.

The smile on Jesus' face warmed Peter. "One fish. The first you catch. Open its mouth and you will find a coin, a shekel. That will pay for you and me."

Peter went to the seashore without hesitation and without the least doubt. He knew he would catch a fish. He knew it would have a coin in its mouth. Jesus had said so. And Jesus was not the man to send anyone on a fool's errand. He caught a pike without any trouble. It wasn't a particularly big one. But it had the shekel in its mouth. It had probably been waiting there for him, swimming around and around until he should keep the rendezvous arranged by Jesus. It had probably refused the bait offered by less fortunate fishermen, saving its money for Peter.

Only a man in a lighthearted mood could think of such a nice way of entertaining a friend—and at the same time such an original way of earning money. But only a man endowed with the power of almighty God could have made the thought come alive. "If we needed two shekels," Peter thought, "that same fish would have had them."

He noticed the tax collector looked a little less hostile when he took the coin, and a little more human.

"So you're a fisherman," the man said.

"How did you know?" Peter demanded, instantly on the defensive.

"The coin smells like fish," the other answered. He eyed Peter with something like respect, and Peter was glad he hadn't said what was in his mind. The man meant well. "You must be a good fisherman," he observed, "or a lucky one. For there's seldom any money in fish."

Peter laughed so hard the man thought he had said something funny. He laughed with Peter. "I could tell you a story," Peter said, "but the trouble with fish stories is that nobody believes them. Suppose I told you a fish paid me that shekel to save his life; and that I threw him back into the sea when I took his money!" He walked away laughing.

May

The Story of Slug
St. Joseph the Worker
May 1

A story my friend Father Ferguson told me recently has made me think of my old friend, Slug. His name was Lewandowski. Ed Lewandowski. But nobody ever called him any name but Slug. He lived far down on the south side of Chicago. He was a war veteran.

He called himself Slug because he considered himself nothing but a sluggard. After he had injured a leg in a railroad accident, on the way home from World War I, he had been forced to stay in bed—twenty-five years or so!

He offered his pain, his helplessness and loneliness as a sacrifice for sinners, as a "voluntary victim." He suffered agonies in reparation for sins—his own and others. And he was always asking Catherine or me to tell him a funny story.

Usually only Catherine was home when he phoned. Catherine knew, the moment she recognized his voice, that he was in desperate pain. She wanted to rush to him, but he was miles and miles away. She rushed to him anyway, making her voice dance with happiness. She is like that.

"Why, Slug! How wonderful you called. I was just thinking about you. How are you?"

He was alone in the second-floor flat, in the rear. His wife, Rose, was at work. Rose worked all day so she could keep him

And she tended him assiduously all the rest of the time. It was hard to say which was the real sufferer, the real voluntary victim, Slug or his wife.

Slug would laugh, hearing Catherine's greeting; but she knew that his face was twisted with agony. And it was probably a dirty white. And it was wet. Yet his eyes would be shining. He was always like that when the pain was worst.

She knew too that his thin moist hair would be sticking up on top, like that of a Kewpie doll. Mrs. Slug had a Kewpie doll she kept on the dresser. She had saved it from her girlhood. She often said she had saved it only because it looked like Slug.

When he was at his worst, Catherine would ask, "You want me to tell you a story?" Her voice then would be as soft as though she were talking to a child.

"Funny stories, Katie my pal," Slug would beg. "I'm a little worse than usual today. I've got to have strength. I've got a big job to do, a very big job."

That meant, we knew, that he was offering up his suffering to bring some sinner back to the sacraments, to soften some hard heart, to let the light burst into some dark mind, to change some wretch's life.

The choking in Slug's voice, the fight for breath, the struggle for control, the battle to keep from screaming! Was Christ like that, we wondered, when he stood at the pillar and let himself be scourged? Was there this same sound of laughter, and of torture, in the whistle of the whips, in the smack of thong on flesh, in the sibilant curses of the scourgers, in the jeers of those who watched?

"Christ, give him strength," Catherine would pray. And then she would laugh again, heartily, merrily. "Did I tell you the latest about Eddie?"

"If it's about Eddie it must be good," Slug would say.

I was the butt of all the jokes, the comic character to whom everything unfortunate happened. Catherine would make up something, anything, elaborate it, embellish it, wash it down with ripples of gay laughter. "Oh," Slug would say, "that's wonderful, wonderful. Poor Eddie!"

Was it possible, we sometimes asked each other, that Christ, in the garden, when the bloody sweat burst through the pores of his holy flesh—as the moisture now was seeping through Slug's cheeks—was it possible that Christ wanted at least one of his apostles to wake and tell him something funny so that he might the better return to his bitter chalice? Was that why he went to them in the night? (Mt 26:36-45).

"Slug—shall I pray for you? Shall I pray that you be released from this torture?" Sometimes the words escaped her.

Slug always answered that she was not to pray for him. Nobody was to pray for him—unless it was to help him stand the pain God sent him. A good story was like a prayer to Slug. It helped him stand the pain.

Any story would help him. Slug was a simple man. He could not understand subtleties. There was not an ounce of sophistication in him. He was only a boy who had marched off to war, to make the world safe for democracy, who had been badly hurt, and who had spent twenty years and more in bed, trying to make the world safe from itself. He had no great sense of humor. His ideas of wit came from the comic strips. A mother-in-law joke was worth a thousand laughs to him. A rolling pin was worth two thousand. He told jokes himself, corny little jokes, and laughed at them as though he had never heard them before.

For ten minutes or so Catherine would talk, and Slug would chuckle—though sometimes there were pauses in his chuckling that were all but impossible to bear. Was it like that when, on the cross, Christ cried out—after a terrible silence—"My God, my God, why have you deserted me?" (Mt 27:46).

Slug would be silent for a time. And then he would say, "It's in the bag, Katie me pal. It's in the bag for sure." That meant that some boy would come back to his mother, some husband would return home, some sinner would die with the last sacraments of the Church.

I said good-by to Slug the day before I came to Canada to live. "So long, Eddie," he said. "Don't drink Canada Dry. It can't be done, you know. It ain't in the bag." Yes, he was that corny!

He died a few weeks after that, on the feast of the Sacred Heart of Jesus. That is the day he would have picked, had he had his choice. And who shall say he did not have his choice?

* * *

Slug, with his gloriously blue popeyes, his Kewpie lock, his corny jokes, his courage, his holy patience—how he would have loved Father Ferguson's story! It isn't a funny story. But it is a strange one. And it is about a saint.

It is about Brother André, the lay brother of the Holy Cross order in Montreal, who worked so many miracles through his friend, St. Joseph; the little man who built the shrine so many thousands of people visit every year.

"The mother superior of a certain convent wanted a janitor," Father Ferguson said, "but she couldn't find one. She went frantic. She advertised. She used employment agencies. She tried everything. There were no janitors out of work. It seemed the convent boiler and the school heating system would not function that year. The nuns and the children would freeze. So, eventually, she came to Brother André, and asked him to pray to St. Joseph on her behalf.

"Brother André advised her to go back to her convent and say her own prayers to the saint.

"About ten days later the good nun came to Brother André again. St. Joseph, she said, had scorned her prayers. She was desperate. The weather was getting colder every day, and there wasn't a janitor in all the North American continent, it appeared. What should she do?

"'How did you pray to St. Joseph?' the brother asked her. 'What did you say to him?'

"The mother superior began, 'O dear St. Joseph, sweet St. Joseph, most worthy St. Joseph—'

"'Faugh!' said Brother André. 'No wonder he didn't listen to you. "Sweet St. Joseph!" He wasn't sweet. He was a hard-working carpenter; and there were occasions when he worked with horses. Sometimes he smelled of the stables. "Sweet St. Joseph!" He was a humble man, a man's man. He doesn't want women slobbering all over him, even holy nuns.

"'Now you go home, cut a picture of St. Joseph out of a newspaper or magazine, put it under the statue of the Sacred Heart, and then say some decent prayers; and you will get a first-class janitor.'

"The good woman did as she was told. But back she came the very next day with another complaint.

"'The janitor came, didn't he?' Brother André demanded.

"'Yes,' mother superior admitted, 'but he's got only one arm. That is, his left arm is cut off just below the elbow. He's a good man. He's an engineer. But he has only one hand. And what can we do with a one-handed janitor?'

"'You are mighty particular,' Brother André commented. 'St. Joseph sends you a janitor and you find fault with him. You didn't send him away?'

"'Not yet, but I'll have to.'

"'You'll keep him,' Brother André said. 'And, incidentally, when you go home and remove the picture from underneath the statue of the Sacred Heart, take a good look at it.'

"I suppose the good nun thought Brother André rude, uncouth, ungentlemanly, un-Christian, and somewhat crazy. Even mothers superior can feel like that, at times.

"Nevertheless she decided to keep the man on, temporarily at any rate; but to keep on trying to find a two-handed janitor. Also, impelled more by curiosity than anything else, she did take the picture of St. Joseph out of its place beneath the statue. And then she saw what Brother André had meant.

"The nun who had cut that picture out of a magazine had been a little careless with her scissors, and had snipped off part of St. Joseph's left arm. She had cut it just below the elbow."

Pistol Pete's People

My wife Catherine had been limping more and more each day. Finally, under duress, she admitted she was in pain. She had hurt her knee, falling off a high rock on the shores of the magic Madawaska River—the same knee she had hurt seriously three years before. I suggested she go to the hospital.

"I didn't go to the hospital three years ago," she said. "Why should I go now? Hospitals cost money, and we are living in holy poverty."

"You are going to the hospital," I told her, "because I say so."

I called a doctor. He examined her knee. And Catherine, still protesting, went to the hospital. "Our Lady will take care of you," I told her.

Then I had to leave her (we were by then in Chicago) and go to Kansas City for a reporting assignment. The morning I returned, I taxied to the hospital. I tiptoed into her room. She was asleep, her head of shining gold hair lying on a pillow. Her arms were outstretched, almost like the arms nailed to the crucifix that lay on the table by her bed.

There was a message for me in the crucifix. It took me a long time, though, to read it: "Those hands once gestured to wind and wave; and wind and wave did as he suggested. They beckoned to Lazarus, stinking in his tomb. And Lazarus came out alive, struggling out of his linen shroud. They touched the sick, the lame, the blind, and healed them all. They have no power now. He permitted us to take it from him. But those hands still hold illimitable measures of love and mercy. Look!"

Whoever carved those hands may have used Catherine's hands as a model.

Catherine woke and blessed me with a smile.

"I was dreaming of you," she said, "and here you are."

She was in pain. But she was also jubilant. And there was something like triumph in her look.

I remembered then that she had always felt it a high privilege to suffer on whatever cross the Lord gave her. In suffering, she might atone for her sins and the sins of others. A living crucifix!

I would have bet all the money I had that she was offering up her torment for those who had tormented her throughout her life. I asked her how she was.

"Really I'm all right," she insisted. "The nurses have been kind to me. And Father Meegan has been in several times."

Father Meegan—"Pistol Pete" everybody called him, for he was always as "keen as a pistol"—was Bishop Bernard Sheil's secretary. He "collected" men and women who had no chance to live long lives, and induced them to offer up their sufferings for the redemption of others. They added their weaknesses, their loneliness, their pain and their prayers to the blood shed by Jesus on the cross, and to the tears shed by his mother at the foot of the cross. They were called victim souls. He loved and cherished them. He spent many hours with them, preparing them for heaven.

I felt a touch of panic. Did Father Pete think Catherine was incurable? But the sheer joy of hearing her voice made my fear lift as she continued to talk. "Father Meegan has asked me to make a beautiful dress for Our Lady out of my pain," she said. Her smile was radiant. And her eyes flashed blue. Bluer than the flash of a bluebird's wing, bluer than bachelor buttons or hyacinths in spring, bluer than all the lakes and rivers and oceans in the world.

"Well, you've made it," I said. "It's a blue dress. And it's beautiful."

Coming Home
Anniversary of Death, Father Eddie Doherty
May 4

How wonderful a man's death can be! A man's death can bring splendor as well as sorrow to all who knew him.

It was a heavenly thrill to turn into the gate of my home in Combermere after such a long absence and to see all the people I love. I know it will be even more heavenly when (and if) I turn into your home, God, and see all my loved ones there.

I was glad to see the river and the early flowers.

Did the abominable snowman dine on clams all winter long? He littered the bed of the river with their shells. They stare up at a man through the clear chill waters, empty, lavender-lacquered, lovely; lying in pleasant disarray on the golden sands.

They present a poignant contrast to the first spring flowers. Their beauty is dead, but will endure for years; the living crocuses will perish in a night.

Yours is the only beauty that never dies, God.

Even now, the unexpected snow flurry falls on them like a shroud.

The greatest thrill came to me in Arizona. We were driving from Tucson toward Prescott and it was still light. We were high up in the mountains on a wide mesa. It looked like the top of the world; I could see your creation all around me. All around me and above me.

I liked the way you had sculpted the mountains in Tucson and the way you draped the sunset colors over them. I liked the saguaro cacti that lifted their arms in prayer everywhere I could see. The sun was sliding slowly down its western slope; and you were illuminating the white and gray clouds with red and gold.

The moon was high in the east, a strange, full moon. The ghost of a moon. A blown dandelion of a moon. A moon a man could almost blow away with his breath, like so much gossamer.

The sun sank out of sight. I watched you mix your oil colors. I watched you smudge them gently with the charcoal powder you use to get your night effects. And I watched you set the sentinel stars.

And I loved you, God, and admired you, and adored you, and thanked you for my life, with all the high points it has known, all the low points, all the sharp points, all the dull points, and all the points that were not points at all, but merely indications of your love and care.

Only for that moment did I love you intensely, God. There have been few such moments in my life.

Perhaps I shall see that dandelion moon again. Perhaps not. It does not matter really, but I shall see you, God, probably, at first, peeking from behind your Mother's skirts and that is the thrill I live for. What other thrill can compare with that?

Combermere—Temporary Heaven
Anniversary of Foundation, Madonna House Combermere
May 17

I have spent nearly a quarter of a century in the midst of saints and saintlings. And this has been the most exciting time of my exciting humpty-dumpty life!

We came to Madonna House, Catherine and I, on May 17, 1947, in a new automobile that looked as big as a locomotive and as expensive as a garage full of Rolls Royces. I had bought it with money borrowed from Bishop Bernard Sheil of Chicago.

We came to a house that was just barely furnished. There were a home-made table, a few home-made chairs, a bed, a stove, and an antiquated pump in the basement that required close to a thousand vigorous up-and-down jerks to supply the upstairs bathroom. There were enough gadgets in the kitchen for the two of us; and I think there were a broom and a mop and half a dozen old-fashioned lamps, plus two antique lanterns.

The house was built on a patch of sand, surrounded by weeds. There was no grass. There were no flowers. There were tremendous and glorious red pine trees. And there was the majestic blue Madawaska River, gently kissing the shores on two sides of us and streaking away from our front steps miles and miles into the unknown!

Getting to Know God

The house was beautiful and strong. It was built with great love and patience by a friend of Catherine's. Even before we married, Catherine told me stories about the house and about Combermere. The village was, among other things, the most peaceful place in the world and the most beautiful.

I visualized the place as I listened to her and felt glad many a time that I would probably never see it. Who wanted to spend any time in a setting like that? Rest and rest! Quit the big cities and be a rustic? Not me. The big cities were my life. My arteries throbbed to their rhythms. I loved their noises, their slums, their canyons, their crowds, their vices and virtues, their different characters.

I loved Chicago. I loved New York. I loved San Francisco, New Orleans, London and Paris, Jerusalem and Rome, Havana and Stockholm. I loved travelling—always at the expense of some magazine or newspaper. I made a lot of money and I loved spending it.

My Russian Catherine changed me, subtly, slowly, in her own delicious way. We hadn't been married long before I found myself—to my utter disbelief and horror—promising to live in "holy poverty" with her. I was the "battleship" in the editorial room of the *Chicago Sun* newspaper. I had a top salary. I was given the best assignments. Everything was going my way. Yet, one day in August 1945, I decided to visit Combermere. Surely, I told myself, I could stand the country for two weeks. I might even make Catherine think I liked it. (That would please her.)

So I entered the house in Combermere and surveyed its cosy loveliness. Then I sat at the home-made table and looked at the Madawaska sparkling in the sun. And I said aloud—again to my disbelief and horror—"I am going to buy this house."

I bought it. It didn't occur to me that I had a promise of poverty. If it occurred to Catherine, she didn't mention it. I had sold a book and Catherine hadn't had time to give all the royalties to her friends, the poor. So the house was mine—ours.

I was crazy! Why did I buy a house? So I could spend two weeks in it every year? Or for some reason I didn't know and never could understand?

The local bishop visited us and asked Catherine to start working with his people in the Combermere area. Catherine promised to do what she could, when she could. But at the time she was director of Friendship House in Chicago. And I was working in Chicago full-time.

I had learned to be uneasy whenever Catherine began to talk business with a bishop. Bishops had ways of changing a man's life. I could testify to that.

A year later the *Chicago Sun* found itself in such a financial mud-hole that it had to get rid of three hundred or more of its highest salaried people. About the same time Catherine came to the agonizing decision that she should resign as director of Friendship House and go to Canada to help the rural poor.

The *Sun* gave me severance pay, which Catherine gave to her poor in Chicago. The day came when we had nothing but the furniture in our Chicago flat, the clothes we wore, and the house in Combermere.

We didn't have money enough for bus fare. So we bought that big automobile with the bishop's money and a loan from a priest friend of mine. We loaded the car with books, a reproduction of the picture of Our Lady of Guadalupe, and all the cooking utensils and dishes we had.

We arrived in Combermere sometime in the afternoon. I remember the bullfrogs that kept me awake most of the evening and the birds that woke me early in the morning. I remember the first time I dug a ditch in which to plant rhubarb and almost broke my back. I remember the days when I was trying to write enough books to keep us alive and everybody in the countryside came to interrupt me—"Where's the Baroness? Where's Catherine? Where's the B? Where's the nurse? My wife is going to have a baby, where's your wife?"

We were all alone, just the two of us. No money coming, no money in the house. Eventually, one of the original Friendship House staff workers, Grace Flewelling, came to live with us. People began to send money and clothes and furniture and even food. Neighbors brought us buckets of wild strawberries or the hindquarters of a deer. God was good to us. So were people.

Strangely enough, I never tired of the new life forced upon me. I agreed with Catherine that Canada was one of the most beautiful countries in the world and that our section was lovelier than any other.

I loved the people. I loved their hospitality, their honesty, and their constant offer to help in any way they could. I loved the river and the dirt roads and the tall, strong-scented pines and the little bits of feldspar that greeted me with such vivid flashes of color when the sun shone on them.

I had expected to be horribly bored in Canada, away from all the people and all the things that had helped make up my life, away from all ambitions, plans, hopes, and aspirations I had cherished—and abandoned.

But, to my ever-growing amazement, I found that this back bush wilderness was the most exciting and fascinating place I had ever known!

Look at that orange butterfly spreading its wings wide above that purple thistle! Look at those jewelled dragonflies lying in the sun on the bosom of a water lily! Looking at beauty is looking at God. What could be more exciting than that?

I realized that God had taken me out of Chicago only to place me in a paradise. I realized that I no longer loved a man-made city; that I was infatuated by a "brand new" God-made world. I realized also that this particular world, attractive and vital as it was, was also a desert—my own particular desert.

I was a stranger here. I would always be a stranger. I was practically a hermit. A hermit without a permit; but a hermit just the same. Me, the gabby gadabout, the newspaperman who always had to be where the shooting was. I had become a hermit! And, what was sillier still, I loved it! I was free at last. I was at peace. I had nothing whatever to do except to love God and all his creatures and to trust in him for everything I needed.

I felt this most keenly after my trip to the Pembroke General Hospital in 1948. I was supposed to have had a coronary thrombosis. But the doctor said it was a mere infarction and that my heart was good for thirty years at least. I tried to bargain with him for forty years, thirty-five, thirty-four. He was adamant. No more than thirty. Why should any man want more?

I came home in a few days but I was weak for many months—too weak to dig in the garden, to shovel snow, to help Catherine in any way. There were days when I couldn't even lift a newspaper! So I stayed lying down on one of those store-bought city-slicker things and watched the world march through the seasons.

It was there, I think, that I knew God wanted me to spend the rest of my life in the Madonna House Apostolate. It was there I began to watch heaven working on the young men and women who had come to see "what Madonna House was all about." They submitted to the work in awe but with some reluctance at first. After a while they cooperated eagerly. They accepted the love they found in Madonna House. They decked themselves in it. They began to love.

Love transfigured them, made their eyes shine, made them sing, made them laugh, made them work as though they were being paid an ounce of gold for every hour. Nobody was ever paid for anything in Madonna House. Nobody ever worked harder anywhere in the world than the staff workers of Madonna House. They worked for the sheer love of God and the love of each other. Catherine kept saying, "Love one another—love one another—love one another."

It was there I watched the first staff workers marching through the seasons of God. No newspaper story I have ever covered held such wonder, such suspense, such triumph.

It was there I began to see that my job was to keep out of Catherine's way—not to interfere with her management of the house and the apostolate. All I had to do was to stay in my hermitage. God and Our Lady would help her more than I could. I could trust them. I should trust them. I did trust them. So what did I have to worry about?

Without any aid from me, Madonna House grew and grew and grew. People came from the ends of the earth—some to stay for a while, some to give it their lives. Donations multiplied. We kept building because everything we built became too small too soon. More and more people came.

Father John T. Callahan came to preach a retreat and stayed to become our first chaplain and later on the director general of the priests.

Madonna House began to flower. Bishops came from east and west, north and south, to ask for help. We began to establish Madonna Houses in many parts of the world.

We continued to build. We built a chapel, then two chapels. We built dormitories. We added acres to our small original property. Now we have more houses and dormitories in Combermere and a dozen other parts of the world than any hermit ever dreamed of having.

So although I am a hermit and live in a desert, it is a temporary heaven. We all live in temporary quarters. Someday the Lord will transfer us to a permanent place. May it be heaven! See you there!

June

More Than a Statue
Our Lady of Combermere
June 8

Our Lady, the Mother of Jesus, took complete charge of Madonna House. We had consecrated ourselves completely, through her, to her Son. She made it grow and prosper. Our numbers increased. Our activities multiplied. Our neighborhood widened constantly until it took in all the world.

Our scanty five acres were multiplied by her and came to include an amazing farm. Our six-room house she turned into a veritable village, complete with several chapels. She brought caravans of trucks and vans to us, with donations of all kinds, to give away. Some of these we sell, with all the proceeds going to the missions.

She gave us so many blessings, we began not to think of them as miracles, or anything strange or unusual or out of the ordinary. We took all her gifts for granted. We walked on the water of her thoughtfulness and care, and never realized our feet were dry.

One of the nicest of her gifts is the bronze statue that stands near the grove of red pines close to the road. It's almost impossible to explain her presence there. Some woman in Chicago prayed to Our Lady of Combermere, and received a tremendous favor. She almost demanded we put up a statue of her at Madonna House and she promised money to cover the cost. But why?

Getting to Know God

There had been no apparitions, no visions here. There had been no spectacular cures. But the statue came. It was sculpted by Miss Frances Rich of Santa Barbara, California. Remember the regal beauty Irene Rich, one of the early movie stars? Frances is her daughter, one of the most distinguished sculptors in the world. She gave the exquisite heroic size Virgin to Madonna House, and had it sent to Florence, Italy to be cast in bronze.

It arrived in the fright yard of Barry's Bay, alone in a box car, on April 26, 1960, the feast of Our Lady of Good Counsel, and was erected May 17, 1960, the thirteenth anniversary of our arrival in Combermere. On June 8, our bishop, the Most Rev. W. J. Smith, gave it his blessing and made it the newest shrine in all Christendom.

He said, "We bless and dedicate the diocese, and the country, and all the Americas, to Our Lady of Combermere. Graces will flow, going out in abundance from Our Lady of Combermere and we shall all benefit from this center of the lay apostolate.... We hope that God will continue through the hands of Our Blessed Mother, the dispenser of all graces, to bless this hallowed spot and make it memorable in the social doctrine of the Church."

In one way, Our Lady of Combermere is like the Pilgrim Virgin, the statue of Our Lady of Fatima, which our friend Father Pat Moore carries around the world; and various laymen carry from parish to parish in Chicago, and other big cities, as escorts of honor.

"You never feel she's just a statue," Jim McNamara of Chicago told me. "You know, of course, that it's only a statue," Jim went on, "but it is impossible not to feel you are in Our Lady's presence all the time you're with her."

"She's only a statue," Father Moore said, "but nobody feels idiotic if he talks to her. She's more than a statue the whole world over."

Spring Wild Flowers

A group of children coming home from school some weeks ago darted into the woods as I came along the road toward them. I thought, naturally, that my appearance had frightened them. I may as well confess that I sometimes go two full days without shaving. But I was giving myself an importance I did not rate. They hadn't paid any attention to me. They were neither frightened by me nor aware of me. They were hunting wild flowers.

One little girl, with her hands filled with red flowers, cried out to another, "Trilliums!" Her chum, carrying a great bunch of white and yellow flowers, said, "And I got stars!"

Gold and silver stars. Dark red triangles. And everywhere—so numerous the children disregarded them—were violets in all shades of blue and purple.

Odd where these beautiful things grow. In the rotten wood of a tree that fell a hundred years ago or more. In patches of brambles. In the shade of a broken birch. In inaccessible places, and in spots where the black flies and the mosquitoes are so thick even the most intrepid do not venture there.

You can't see the flowers from the roadside, though you can sniff their fragrance. You've got to get into the woods and stoop and crawl and proceed with the utmost caution everywhere to collect a fistful.

Sometimes you get the silly idea that even God, who planted them, can't find them, doesn't want to look for them, has forgotten all about them. And sometimes you think maybe God sent his lightning or his wind to fell that tree a hundred years ago so that its rottenness in time would be good for the roots of that exquisite star anemone, and maybe he snapped that stately birch in two so that its hanging part might afford shelter to this frail maroon triangle.

Do you think that's too much trouble for God to go to—for a couple of wild flowers? It's no trouble at all. And, I suspect, since he uses such exceeding skill to give the flowers beauty, that he loves wild flowers.

You find some people like that too, men and women formed by the cunning hand of God. You come across them in the country wildernesses and in the city's slums. People of fragrant virtue. Hidden saints. Shut-ins, some of them; or invalids who bear affliction with patience, even with joy, because it is the will of God they suffer. You find them if you hunt for them. But they are rare anywhere.

Sometimes you get the crazy idea that God has forgotten them too, or cannot find them. And then you think that maybe even before So-and-so was born God decided this was the soil she needed most, the soil of suffering. Maybe God sent lightning and the winds of adversity to prepare the way for her. What fragrance she will bring him!

The children whom I saw in the woods intended to place their trilliums and their gold and silver stars before the statue of Our Lady. I wouldn't be surprised to learn that God picks his human wild flowers with the same object in mind. To place them before his mother. That she may enjoy them forever.

Not Your Average Wife
Wedding Anniversary
Eddie and Catherine Doherty
June 25

Thank you for women, Lord. Thank you for all wives; all wives, everywhere. What would we do without them? And every wife, I suppose, is as beautiful to her husband as mine is to me.

When the average wife starts the story like this—"I was really going slow, not more than forty, when I heard this funny noise under the hood"—the average husband gets the dreadful and true idea of how the story—and the car—will end. "Well, it's no use crying over spilt milk or a split Mercedes; time to get a new clunker anyway."

His Holiness, Pope Pius XII, had summoned all the leaders of lay movements—Catholic Action—to attend a special congress in Rome. While there, Catherine had had a private audience with the pope, and had now rejoined me in Paris.

So when Catherine began the story of her audience with the pope, by mentioning how she had met Monsignor Montini, the Papal Secretary of State, I was alarmed.

She was not the average wife. She never pulled a punch. She had been a newspaperwoman and knew she must put the punch line in the first paragraph. She knew though, that there are some stories in which you keep the punch line to the very last. This one was going to be a knockout!

We were in Paris, at an outdoor cafe, and I sat, pretending not to listen, but hearing every word Catherine uttered.

"Monsignor Montini arranged an audience for me with the Holy Father himself. Can you imagine that?"

"This is going to cost you plenty," I thought to myself.

"Montini sympathized with me and wanted to be a friend," Catherine continued. "I told him all about myself, my ideas, my aims, my plans. And what I thought about secular institutes." (A secular institute is an organization of people who live in the world and consecrate their lives in a special way to God through the life and work of their institute. Members retain their occupations, and profess poverty, chastity and obedience.)

"Pope Pius loves secular institutes," Catherine said. "People like us, you and I, can take vows of poverty, chastity and obedience, the counsels of perfection! And still remain lay men and women! Isn't that sublime, Edward J.?"

Sublime, yes. It would be sublime to take a vow of chastity, but Catherine was my wife! How could I give her up?

Secular institutes. The words were shovels digging into sand and dirt and gravel; and dirt and sand and gravel were falling on a plain box six feet below the snow and ice. I was going to lose Catherine to a secular institute.

Maybe she doesn't mean it, I thought. But I knew damn well she did. So what was I going to do?

God didn't promise me anything. He didn't talk to me. But the sword was in my heart. It went in without any pain. No pain at all, but a sharp stab of joy!

"No distinctive habits," Catherine was saying. "The kids can still smoke cigarettes and use lipstick and mascara, and wear cheap jewelry. We shall have a few rules in our apostolate, but lots of love...."

There was no pain! Only joy!

It didn't make sense!

Once, when Catherine was new and strange to me, I heard her tell a frigid woman that "sex is the chalice of the Sacrament of Marriage; without it, there is no sacrament. Without it there is no marriage."

Catherine was the very bread and wine of the sacrament, its carnal ecstasy and its spiritual exaltation. And I had surrendered her—just like that?

I looked at her. Her face was lit with wonder and with holy joy. And her blue eyes were wet with tears.

Fire is a mystery, I thought. Water is a mystery. Wind is a mystery. Earth is a mystery. Light and darkness are mysteries. But love is the greatest mystery of all.

God can place himself in a snowflake, or a grain of sand, or a mustard seed, or a woman's eyes, so that love and faith and the sort of wisdom owned by children and fools like me can find him.

You know what color God is? God is blue. God is bluer than the bluest of all blue skies.

"Lord," I breathed, "the chalice you gave to me and Catherine the day we married is still filled with your holy and heady wine. We lift it to you, and return it to your altar. We too have kept the best wine for the last.

"When you gave me Catherine you blessed me, and you gave me joy. When you take her from me, you not only bless me again and let me keep the joy but also you increase it. But what will life be without her? Shall I know hunger and thirst again? Shall I again live with loneliness, and without music and incense and spice? And without the sun and the moon and all the big and little stars? So be it!

"Was the wine sweet in the chalice you Son drank in the Garden of Olives? It was bitter, wasn't it? Why is this wine so wondrous sweet?" Never ask God why. Even if he tells you, you cannot possibly understand.

My mind detoured back to Rome as Catherine talked, back to early Rome, back to the days of the first Christians who died for Christ. Which death would a Christian choose, supposing he had the choice? The panther or the plague? The cancer or the cougar? The wild bull, the lion, or the pox?

Catherine and I had been given a choice the early Christians never had. We could give up more than our lives. We could give not only ourselves; we could also give each other!

I lit her cigarettes, mechanically, beating the waiter to it every time. I sipped the liquid in front of me, and acted like any other American in Paris as she talked on and on about her meeting with the pope.

I summoned the waiter, just to have something to do, and ordered us another drink. Around us were the passing crowds of Paris. If the city's soul was reflected in the faces of these people, the citizens, the tourists, the police, the peddlers, the prostitutes, the beggars, it was the most wonderful place in the world for a holy honeymoon!

"Millions of people in this anthill, and all the other anthills on earth," I ventured, "are going about their daily chores as if nothing important has ever happened to them, or ever will. But you and I, in the little while we have been here, have experienced something so infinitely wonderful that we can never be the same again."

"Heaven has stooped to our nothingness," she said, "to let us know it wants that nothingness.

"We are in God's hands, and he asks a gift of us, a priceless gift, the rarest gift on earth. How can we possibly be the same again?

"What life can be prosaic that has heard and heeded the lyric voice of God?"

Catherine kept talking, but I don't believe either of us heard a word she said. We kept looking at each other a long, long time, realizing we had made a decision!

Each of us, at the same time, had fallen on the sword of the holy will of God, and was stabbed with an unearthly joy!

An hour before I would have said, "My life, Lord, yes; take it and welcome. My wife, no! Not again!" But, without saying a word, I had already given her to God, and she had given God me!

There was not the slightest feeling of separation in either of us. Rather, we felt closer together than we had when we sat down to eat and drink and talk. The swords had pinned us together heart to heart, and soul to soul, forever. How can a man explain such a thing?

"It's foolishness doubled and redoubled," I said.

"The folly of the cross," she replied.

"So when do we take the vows?" I asked.

"First we must see how the Madonna House staff feels about it. Then we must go about the business of organizing our apostolate according to Church law. We have to have a constitution, get approval, do a lot of things. Rome never moves fast. It may be many years before we are ready."

Years! God was merciful. He might even let me escape before Rome got around to okaying Madonna House as a secular institute. "I'm in no hurry," I said. "let God take his time. Don't rush him."

We paid the waiter, and I probably told him to keep the change. I was in that sort of mood. It was a jubilant day in the most beautiful and happy city God had ever made! And we walked, hand in hand, through the streets of Paris, enjoying the honeymoon of all honeymoons.

But just before we left the table, I refilled our glasses. We tinkled them together in a sort of toast, then set them down, untouched.

* * *

That memorable day in Paris was a birthday in the spirit of Christ, the spirit of renunciation, and in the unexpected joy of doing the will of God instead of my own. I do not remember exactly what day it was. But I remember distinctly that it was some time later, in the evening of the sixty-fifth anniversary of my birthday, on October 30, that Catherine and I knelt on the floor of my room in Madonna House, and took promises of poverty, chastity and obedience, in the presence of Father John Callahan and Father Eugene Cullinane, priests of Madonna House.

"Now," Catherine said, "we can love as the blessed souls love in heaven, where there is 'neither marrying nor giving in marriage.' Much more than yesterday, and much less than tomorrow."

I had fallen in love with her all over again; yet I did not call her back that night when she went across the river to the house we had called St. Catherine's. Instead, I went slowly up the steps to my empty room above the kitchen.

And the words came to me that night.

"Love is crucifix and crucified. Sing Our Lady a song of love! Did you think the cross was made of wood alone? Your cross, and Catherine's is but the difference you are apart. Loved and lover are crucified on the same cross, you on one side, she on the other, the cross of love! Sing Our Lady a hymn of thanks!

"You think of unity and closeness as if you were a man without a song. To you and Catherine, the Lord has opened a unity beyond the dreams of any who cannot sing. He has given you two the gift of loving the way he loved.

"Lift up your voice and sing!

"His gift is the privilege to live, here on earth, as you may do in heaven. He gives you, in time, his kingdom of eternity. Open your heart and sing. Sing a song of glory and of joy."

In my heart that night, I sang with joy and glory.

July

July. School is closed. The black flies have disappeared, bad cess to them. May they never come back! And the wild flowers that came with the spring have vanished too. The year's more than half gone! Before long, it'll be snowing again.

Posthole Passion

Canada Day
July 1

Gid was a great fisherman, a mighty hunter, the guide of many tourists in the spring and fall, and the greatest and most lovable liar in the land.

He loved to tell stories as he sat around the campfire at night cooking dinner, gutting fish, or maybe skinning a deer. He spoke to make the men around him feel kinship with one another. The stories they tell of him are many.

"How do you spell *squirrels*" one of his clients asked him.

"One *i* and two *r's*," another man replied.

A red-faced man, a wealthy Cleveland lawyer, took exception to that remark.

"The squirrel has two eyes, everybody knows. Look at those two in the elm tree over there. Each of them has two eyes."

"How much do you want to bet?" Gid asked. "The female has no right eye and the husband no left."

The lawyer laughed at him.

"How can you tell the female from the male at this distance?"

"Which one is doing all the scolding?" Gid asked him.

"Get your gun and bring 'em both down," the lawyer said; "bet you twenty dollars each has two eyes."

"You're covered," Gid said, and said "bang, bang" with the gun.

The squirrels dropped down at his feet.

"The twenty bucks is mine," he said. "You see, this squirrel has no right eye, this one no left."

The lawyer laughed and put the money into Gid's hand.

"I bet you fifty you can't do that again," he said.

"Mister," Gid replied, "we don't waste squirrel meat around here. These two will make a stew that will last us for the next three days."

* * *

Gid served his country in two wars. When he was buried in the summer of '63, a number of old soldiers paid last honors to their comrade.

Gid Rose, old soldier, old hunter and trapper, old fisherman and guide, old friend and neighbor, had one particular lie he loved to tell. It was buried with him.

At the end of the day when the fish had not been biting, or the deer had not come near them, he loved to sit the men down and spin his lies to their delight.

To every new batch of men he guided, he told with proper gestures the story of his posthole joys and sorrows.

"Them postholes used to lie around loose everywhere and I was always worrying about 'em. Postholes deteriorate if a man don't take care of 'em.

"You can't bring 'em inside the house. There's no room for 'em. You gotta leave 'em outside.

"It's tough to sit up all night with a lantern and watch over 'em like a shepherd over his sheep.

Getting to Know God

"Rain and snow and dead leaves and loose stones can get into 'em.

"Sometimes dogs sniff around 'em. Sometimes a passing skunk stops to say 'hello' to 'em."

Fish were frying as Gid talked. Twigs were sputtering and snapping in the campfire. Smoke was blending with the dusk. Gid was standing tall and straight and solemn, holding a fork in his powerful right hand, squinting a little—because of the smoke—at the men sitting all around him listening to his talk.

"No, I didn't mean to put fenceposts in 'em holes. Don't need a fence. I collected 'em like some of you fellas collect dollar bills.

"Posthole crazy! But, easy come, easy go.

"Man goes to sleep a posthole millionaire, and wakes to find himself a beggar.

"One night, while I was dreaming about owning all the postholes in Canada, a wind blew up and filled every one of my holes with sand.

"Couldn't identify a one of 'em. I was wiped out!"

"What did you want to do with your postholes, anyway," someone was sure to ask.

"You never know when them holes will come in handy. Get enough of 'em together, you can make yourself a tunnel, or a well, or a mine, or, maybe, for all I know, a lot of foxholes or a couple of miles of trenches."

Gid Rose was a living symbol of Canada.

He had its majesty, its strength, its bigness, its grace, its rugged honesty, its sublime simplicity, its wealth of energy, all of its gaiety and fun.

He didn't die broke. He still had his postholes.

He had as many postholes as he had medals on his uniform jacket, enough to furnish him a deep and wide and comfortable and everlasting grave.

Take care of him, Lord.

He was, in his own way, one of the most religious men I knew. He loved your great out-of-doors.

Introduce him to Peter, Lord, and let them talk about the fish they caught and the fish that got away.

Where the Wild Strawberries Grow

Dear God of Heaven and Earth,

Do you remember July 1 a few years ago? I was walking through your woods in Combermere that morning. I had a long stick and with it I broke off the dead branches of the poplar trees.

I broke them off because they barred my way. The poplar starts branching when it is scarcely more than a twig. It has no mother to guide it.

When it grows a little it discovers it doesn't need the lower limbs. It lets them dry up and die. The mere touch of a stick will break them off.

"God," I said, "many dead branches bar my way to you. Break them. Break everything that keeps me from getting close to you—or you from coming close to me—as I beat a path through the poplar trees of my years.

"Break off my attachments to earthly things, if they come between us. Peanut butter. Lobsters. Ripe cheeses. Hamburger sandwiches. Hot dogs with real English mustard. Bacon. Detective stories. Good books and movies. Comfortable shoes. Leisure. Fancy shirts and ties, Lord. And anything else.

"Smash all the dead wood in me, the branches I was so proud of in my youth and middle age, the twigs that shaped my life—and shut you out of it.

"Smash the live wood too, Lord, if it displeases you.

"Strip me of all my faults and let the dead lumber fall where it will—to be as forgotten as my sins."

I watched the poplars and the pines adoring you, lifting their arms to you, whispering, "Holy, Holy, Holy!"

There were ponds of Our Lady's paintbrush everywhere, red and orange flowers. I watched them bowing and prostrating themselves before you. They rippled with the excess of their love, singing your praises silently. They looked like pools of fire and their fragrance filled the world.

I saw the wild roses climb their vines to get a better look at you and your Mother, our Mystical Rose. They hoped you might reach down and give them a friendly pat. They blushed with their young love.

I saw the daisies, with the faces of happy nuns, blow ardent kisses to you as they curtsied in the winds.

I saw the buttercups lift to you their chalices of lacquered gold.

And I saw the humble, wild, white morning glories creeping forward through the sparkling dew. They came to touch your blessed feet and to chant their morning prayers with their lovely pure throats, which you had shaped to the likeness of the old-fashioned phonograph horns.

Lord, in your mercy, purge me unmercifully, so that when I too come to kneel at your feet I may be as acceptable as those white flowers; and that I may have more to offer you than pale regrets.

A partridge shot out of the ferns and a flock of small brown warblers ascended with him. (Did I break up a prayer meeting of the birds?) I thought of the partridge as a missile with the power and the speed of an Our Father exploding in your heart. I thought of the little birds as so many Hail Marys and Glory Bes rushing up to you.

I put a prayer on every flower and every wing. A simple prayer: "I love you."

I picked some of the wild strawberries you had placed on the hillside for me. They were fresh from your hands, fragrant with your divinity, sweet with your breath.

My mother used to say, "God doubtless could have made a better berry, but God doubtless never did." I think it was a quotation. She picked berries with me in Wisconsin, Lord, when

I was a boy. God, tell my mother I thought of her in connection with wild strawberries—and with you. She'll like that.

The strawberry gives it sweetness joyfully. My fingers were red with the juice of the strawberries. I licked them clean.

* * *

"O taste of the Lord and see that he is sweet."

Is that the way it goes? Not quite?

I thought of the Precious Blood of your Son.

You are as generous with the Blood, Lord, as you are with your berries. You have placed it everywhere for us your children, to sweeten our lives, to make us strong and holy.

You permitted it to dye the rocks in the Garden of Olives, the marble floors in Pilate's hall, the wood of the cross, and the soil of Calvary.

Yet it is still offered for us in half a million Masses every day throughout the world!

"O taste of the Blood of God and see that it is sweet!"

(I offer my blood too. Such as it is, Lord, such as it is.)

"O taste and see that the Lord is sweet."

That evening, in my room, I looked in the New American Bible, the Confraternity Edition. I also looked in the Gideon Bible I stole, years ago, from a hotel in Santa Barbara.

I found in both the words, "O taste and see that the Lord is good" (Ps 34:8).

In the Catholic book these words followed: "Blessed is the man who flees to him for safety." And in the other I found, "Blessed is the man that trusts in him."

Somehow, God, I think I would rather trust in you than flee to you for safety—though perhaps it comes to the same thing in a theological argument.

I hope I never have to flee to you for safety. I want to stay in your presence forever.

When I broke off the branches of the poplars, Lord, I was trying to get closer to you. It seems you have been away from me so long!

There are times when you take some little one by the hand, lead him through green pastures, sit him beside still waters, and fill him with your sweetness.

There are other times when you make him walk alone, without you, that he may learn to be a man.

Thank you, God, for letting me come close that day during July, the month of your Son's Most Precious Blood. Thank you for the sweetness of that hour with you.

Whether I walk alone again, or once more hand-in-hand with you, let me keep loving you. Let me keep trying to come closer and closer to you.

I give you the confidence of Job, the confidence of a child. "Though you slay me, yet will I trust in you" (Jb 13:15).

Oh yes—and thank you for the full moon that night and the bracing coolness of the river.

And give my love to Mary and all my friends in purgatory and heaven.

Lady at the Golden Door
U.S. Independence Day
July 4

I keep remembering things Catherine said about America when I first met her. She had loved Abe Lincoln ever since she had read about him and his love for the slaves and for all mankind. "Charity for all," she liked to quote. "Malice toward none." And she loved the words of Emma Lazarus engraved on the Statue of Liberty. "Give me your tired, your poor; your huddled masses yearning to breathe free. The wretched refuse of your teeming shore; send them to me. I lift my lamp beside the golden door."

I have looked at that statue hundreds of times and always with emotion. In my early days as a newspaperman in New York I was often sent out to meet some incoming liner to interview some world celebrity aboard. And at such times I spent hours looking at some of the humbler passengers as they passed the statue. Some of them wept at the sight. Some of them embraced and kissed and danced as though they had seen the hand of Our Lady or Our Lord and had been forever blessed.

In 1919 I was sent by the *Chicago Tribune* to welcome the Illinois troops coming home from Europe after World War I. Early one morning another reporter and I hired a motor boat to take us out to the fleet which was anchored in the bay awaiting the sunrise to come in. We wanted exclusive interviews for our papers. We were sincerely and joyously welcomed—the first American civilians those boys had seen in two years. And how they laughed at our straw hats!

We passed the Statue of Liberty in the full splendor of dawn.

"There she is," one boy said. "The old girl herself."

There were hundreds of others there. Maybe thousands. None of them said a single word. But I wish I could show you the way each one looked at that beautiful lady who lifted her lamp beside the golden door.

Lots of people love America, I thought. But nobody loves the country more than those Americans who have left it for a time and have at last come back to it.

I drifted off to sleep with my thoughts, and somehow Our Lady got mixed up in my dreams and my memories and my emotions. She was the Lady with the lamp lifted high above the golden door.

She was the great lover of America and Americans, a nation and a people dedicated to her Immaculate Conception. She was the Lady holding a light to guard all the tired, the poor, the homeless, the tempest-tossed, the refuse of our teeming shores, into the coziness and the warmth and the shelter and the love of the palace of her Father and her Son and her Holy Spouse.

Hail Mary, full of grace! Hail Lady of the lamp! Pray for us now and at the hour of darkness when we need the light to see the way home.

God's Humor

Lord, everybody besieges you all day and all night, asking for favors, begging for mercy, praising you, blessing you, adoring you.

I too.

No one needs mercy more than I.

No one so needs all the graces you offer.

But once in a while, I have to tell you a joke or make some idiotic wise crack, hoping you will laugh.

I know you have a sense of humor, God, for you created it.

I imagine you would laugh at us most of the time, if you were not so sorry for us and so concerned about us.

And if I feed you only the poorest corn when I dare to jest with you, it is because corn is all I have.

You did not spurn the widow's mite. You will not scorn my corn.

In the woods today I saw a shabby, weary, bleary crow and a nasty little red squirrel.

The bird, roosting high on an old white pine, leered and sneered at me. The squirrel jittered and jibbered and jeered. He was querulous, scurrilous, squirrelous.

(Lord, lift me from the quicksands of this silly mood, but not until I ask, "Why does a crow roost and a rooster crow?")

A black and white butterfly made me forget the intolerant squirrel and the too tolerant crow. And a display of goldenrod made me forget the butterfly.

As I started to the goldenrod, I saw an exciting shade of red, low down beneath a blackberry vine. I thought it was a mushroom, but it was a strawberry leaf.

How often, Lord, how extremely often, your strawberry leaves fool me in my hunt for mushrooms!

Yet I am not vexed at this. Suppose I had not seen the lively color of those leaves! Suppose you had not blessed me with these eyes!

I picked the strawberry plant and studied it, standing a long time, a feast for deer flies and mosquitoes.

I considered, for a moment, the idea of gathering all the bright strawberry banners around me and making them into a garland for Our Lady.

You sang to me, God, as I held that three-leafed strawberry glory in my fingers. I do not know the words, if you used words. But it was about the tints and the mysteries in that trinity of leaves and the same tints and the mysteries in your red-gold sunsets and your gold-red dawns.

And there was something about other trinities.

There is the trinity of root and wood and bark; a trinity of plant and blossom and seed; a trinity of shape and smell and color; a trinity of soil and sun and rain.

There is a trinity of faith, hope and love in my heart and, in my mind, a trinity of intelligence, memory and free will.

Lord, swell my heart so it may contain enough love to spill out on all the world.

Whet my intelligence so it may always know your will.

Strengthen my will so it may always do your will and never mine alone.

Build my memory so it may not forget you, even for a second.

I saw the goldenrod again, a fresh clean spray. Beautiful beyond compare! And full of ants! Lord, is it possible the insects believe this is real gold? How human can ants be?

Here, in the midst of summer, I feel autumn rushing up, the autumn of the life you have given me. After autumn, I will find winter, and my final rest.

And when I close my eyes at last, no more to dream, let the world in which I find myself be filled with your glory and with the radiance and the wonder and the perfume of your mother, "the all holy, the immaculate, the most highly blessed, Our Glorious Lady."

Remember not the shadows of my sinful life. Let there be no shadows when you come.

Getting to Know God

And, if you draw me to you, God, absorb me, hold me, bless me and let my songs, the murmur of a pitiful thin brook, fall gently down, like rain, into dry and shrivelled hearts; into parched and thirsty minds; into wasted and barren souls; that they may be refreshed; that they may laugh and love; that they may bear you fruit.

August

Belly Button Beauty

Lord, I thank you for your gift of love I saw in a beautiful young woman's navel!

She was dressed for the day in halter, shorts and sandals.

The navel was where it should be, right in the middle of her slim, suntanned stomach. It was a beautiful dimple, a delightful gem that only you could make.

Later that day I heard a woman whisper, just loud enough for me to overhear, "Wonder what he thought when he looked at that vulgar, air-cooled navel."

I thought how sensible this woman was to dress according to the day. How nice and cool and innocent she looked, a sight for angels and for men. And also for other women of her age.

I thought of men and women lying on beaches in various parts of the world, looking with love at your water and your sands and your trees and your serene blue skies and at you.

Looking at you, God, and not seeing you at all. Looking at each other, unaware that you were there.

When my brother Tom finishes his weekly letter, he signs it "Editor T." When my brother Bill and other writers finish their copy, they sign it and they add a row of staggering Xs. This is a symbol.

When a painter or an author or a composer finishes a work of art, he puts his name on it.

When a manufacturer has completed his product, he puts it in a container that bears his name. And maybe he stamps it "Made in Japan" or "Made in America" or the name of the place where it was made.

The name or the initials or the symbols of these people mean "Completed—this is good—approved—grade A."

You, God, the Creator, are the Great Artist. You design bodies and souls. You design them in heaven and make them on earth.

Very often in these days vandals break into your holy of holies, your workshop, and ruthlessly destroy your masterpieces.

But, if they permit you to finish your work, you end it at the navel.

You sign it with a beautiful, divine, triumphant flourish of your fingers. And you put a stamp on it which few of us can read.

"Made in heaven for my glory on earth, and your eternal glory with me."

We come not only from your heart, God, but also from your hands. The navel is your signature, your divine okay, your guarantee of life for certain lengths of time, your trademark, your holy name written in the flesh.

> The navel says,
> > "This is a child of God destined for eternal life.
> > "This is a soul and body dear to me.
> > "This is one of my potential saints."

It says, "This body is a work of Divine Love."

It says, "Little children, love one another."

It says, "Souls are born on earth and prepared to take over the kingdom of heaven when the right time comes."

> Lord, you begin your work by creating the soul.
> The soul is the life, the spirit of the body.
> The spark that starts the motor.
> Without a soul there is no life, there is no growth.

Lord, what becomes of the souls who never have been given bodies? What becomes of those who kill the bodies, and thwart the soul?

When I die, please, Lord, make that grand, triumphant flourish of your fingers on my soul.

Give me a new navel for the old and put navels on the souls of all my readers and of all my enemies and friends.

Fishing on the Madawaska

Dear Lord God, Creator of All Things:

We are inclined to take rivers as something to be expected, nothing to get excited about, nothing to mention to the folks at home, unless it's the Tiber or the Nile. Yet rivers, I learned the other day, are really miracles of your loving thoughtfulness, and indications of your power, your wisdom, and your beauty.

There were years in my life when I liked to look at the Chicago River, which is probably the dirtiest stream in Christendom. When I rode the L from Logan Square to the Loop, I put aside the newspaper when we neared the river. I looked down at the slow-moving yellow-gray water, and continued to look at it while the train crossed above it. If it held a boat, I looked at that too. But it was the water that attracted me.

I'll never forget the morning I shoved up the shade in my lower berth, somewhere between Albany and New York, and looked out upon the vast Hudson. It was a serene blue that day, a heavenly blue. I was not exactly on speaking terms with you then, God, but despite myself I lifted my heart to you, in appreciation and in thanks.

I have gazed upon many great rivers since that morning, but none ever thrilled me so much as the Hudson—that is, until I looked upon the Madawaska, which runs in front of Madonna House and winds its way into the mighty Ottawa. This, I think, is the most beautiful river you ever fashioned. It may not compare in importance with the Nile or the Jordan or the Mississippi or the Tiber or the Po; but I like it better every time I look at it; and I look at it a dozen times a day, and maybe a dozen times at night.

I sat in our dining room, the first day I came to Combermere, and stared at the river through the front windows. I didn't believe what I saw. I seemed too lovely to be true. It still seems too wonderful to be real. I have no particular desire to swim in it. I do not want to fish in it. I do not want to go for a boat ride on it. I just like to watch it.

I ventured out on it the other day with your great friend and admirer, Father Callahan, who has become one of the most ardent and skilful fishermen in all the Americas. We went eastward, toward a little bay he knew, a spot where the river is a mile or more wide, and where the River York joins its life.

It was after six o'clock in the evening, but it wouldn't be dark until nine o'clock or so. The sun was veering toward the west, and the river was a more beautiful shade of blue than ever the Hudson was. There are hills along the Madawaska's banks—little mountains—covered with pines and birches. They were soft of outline that evening, those rugged rocky mounds, and soft of color. They blended perfectly with the blue of the water and the sky, and with the gray and white clouds you blew our way.

I let Father Callahan do all the fishing. I didn't touch a rod. I didn't care to do anything but sit in the boat and listen to the song of the outboard motor and look at your water and your mountains and your forests and your clouds. I enjoyed the day, the river, the breeze, the graceful way in which Father Cal cast his line, and the joy with which he coaxed a fish to come and live with him.

I was enjoying you, God!

When I was a boy, and even when I was fifty years old and nearing middle age, I thought prayer was something one did on one's knees, something one said. It was a labor, a duty, even a chore. One prayed because one wanted something. One said morning and evening prayers only because the sisters in Catholic school had taught him to do so, and he had got into the habit and couldn't break it. If he didn't want anything material, then he just wanted to stay on the right side of God—so he wouldn't go to hell.

It had not occurred to me that I could sit silently in a boat, enjoy every minute that passed, drink in all the world around me, be aware of mosquitoes and flies, and still pray ardently to you.

But that's what happened! I suddenly realized that, loving you as I was, I was praying! Who needs words to pray? Who needs anything but love?

Every tree on those hills was praying to you, God. Every little green tip on the pines, every fresh new needle, every fluttery leaf on the spectacular white birches, was praying to you without words. The clouds were praying to you even as they commuted to Toronto or Montreal.

I thought, "God made every one of those trees. He made every little part of them. He knows each one of them. He helps each branch and twig and root to grow. He paints each tiny needle green. He tends to the lovely wallpaper on the birches. He even cares for the rocks and pebbles and the river itself, and everything else, not only here, but throughout the world."

Apparently few people enjoy thinking about you, God. They are afraid of you. They distrust you. They blame you for everything they dislike, for everything they hate. They profess their utter disbelief in you—and they think they do away with you by saying, "There is no God." Whist! Just like that! They pronounce the magic words and God disappears!

The quickness of the hand deceives the eye. The quickness of the hateful heart deceives the mind.

If they enjoy rivers and trees, strawberries and apples and pretty girls, and floating down the river, filling their senses with splendor, then they enjoy you, God.

The sad point is that maybe they don't realize it *is* God they enjoy and not just the people and things you made.

Getting to Know God

I sat there, a long time, just loving and adoring you, God; and watching Father Cal catch fish. Mostly rock bass. Some were too little to keep. He took the hooks from their jaws without touching them with his hands, and let them go back into the water.

I got to thinking about those little fish. And it came to me, there on your blue liquid carpet, God, that you had hooked me firmly and taken me into your boat a long time ago. I was still flopping around like the rock bass Father Cal had decided to keep. And I might flop around for quite a little time.

What I wondered about most, though, was why you hadn't thrown me back! I am a poor sort of fish, not worth anybody's eating—especially yours, God.

I looked at the fish he kept, and remembered two wonderful big-mouthed bass that came out of this same river on one unforgettable occasion.

They were exciting. They fought furiously to stay in the water. The fisherman had to use the net to get them into the boat. They were the most beautiful fish I had ever beheld. I can still see their golden bellies shining in the sun! God, how you use color!

That's the kind of fish I'd like to be, Lord—one that would let everybody see how wonderful you are; you, the Designer and Creator of all beauty.

It was close to nine o'clock when we headed for home. For miles it seemed we were rushing straight into your golden sun. Its light was dazzling, but not blinding. One could look at it and enjoy it.

When my sun sets, Lord, let me come home to you like that, swiftly, steadily, with as much joy in my heart, and with the same prayer, the prayer of love for you and yours. Let there be splendor in my heart and in my eyes, to prepare me for the splendor of your heaven!

Fish came up all around our boat to catch the little flies that skimmed above the still waters. They dropped back into the depths, leaving widening circles that glimmered in the sunlight.

Colors changed to right and left, on the water, on the hills, in the sky, wherever I looked. The great ball of the sun dropped, blushing with its love for you, and painting all the western world of sky and water. An hour later a million stars were swimming in the river.

I am a poor fish, not worth your keeping—but do keep me, God, until you are ready to dispose of me. (Yet keep me clear of the fire!)

Let me, before I end this letter, thank you especially for the Madawaska. You never made a finer river, Lord, unless perhaps you let one flow through Eden.

With all my love,
Your problem child

All You Need Is Love

All that God ever wanted from human beings was love—love of himself and love of neighbor. He gave us everything else. You can't give him money; he owns it all. You can't give him land; he made it all. You can't give him any houses; he gives us all the materials to make them. You can't give him anything he hasn't already got—except love. All he wants is love.

This is what all of us servants of God are trying to do, trying to love God. He made us for no other reason except to love him and one another. How is our work coming along?

* * *

So long as we love one another it doesn't matter too much if we weaken sometimes, if we do things we shouldn't do. Love is the predominant thing between us and God. See that you don't do anything against God or against your neighbor, if that's possible! Love, love, love, love, love—that's what it's all about!

People Aren't Always What They Seem

"Why isn't so and so like us, like decent people!"

We are all prone to judge people by externals—the way they dress, the way they wear their hair, their fancy or awful looking clothes, the way they spend their money.

We think we're so almighty good! We turn up our noses at others we think are no good at all, whereas they just might really be saints for all they endure and suffer in life. Who knows?

What do we really know about alcoholics? They may be very sick; they may have beautiful hearts; they may be ashamed of themselves for drinking; they may be trying to stop.

I've known drunks who were some of the finest people on earth when they were sober. They got drunk, but they couldn't help it, maybe at social gatherings with friends. And I've seen these men come out of their drunkenness and build churches and do wonderfully charitable things in so many ways.

There were a great many such people assisting us in the early days of Madonna House. They did everything they could to make up for their drinking. Like Zacchaeus. Remember him, that little, no-good tax collector in the Bible? After he met Jesus, he gave his money back to the people he had cheated. Afterwards, he was still Zacchaeus, the little man, the tax collector, the sinner, but he had made reparation (Lk 19:1-10).

Now it's all right to be a good Catholic. There's nothing better in the world than to be a really good Catholic! But to look on, say, Protestants, Jews, Muslims, and Hindus as heathens is really outrageous. People are not always what they seem. We will find many of the people we looked down upon in heaven—if we get there! They will be as surprised to see us as we are to see them. I guess we all tend to see others as "beneath us." May God save us all!

September

We Are Trees

The tree of a man's or woman's life will be cut down someday. We are all trees, really. We are born to grow to a certain height. Some of us grow very tall, have a lot of leaves, shade, and fruit. Others are lean and stingy of fruit. Some have no fruit at all. We will be judged accordingly.

What do I mean by having fruit? The things we do, the good things, that's fruit. The things that are a delight to the eye of the Lord and sweet to his mouth. Some trees, apple trees for instance, have so much fruit that they can hardly stand up straight. These are really the prize trees that God loves so much.

We also are full of good fruit, and the Lord loves us very much; he will take care of us. And those who bear no fruit at all, well, it will be a horrible thing to stand before God and not be a delight to his eye and sweetness to his mouth.

At the Foot of the Cross
Our Lady of Sorrows
September 15

I discovered Our Lady, Mary the Mother of God, many years ago when I was a child. I always loved Our Lady and had a devotion to her by the title of Our Lady of Sorrows. I don't know where it came from, but it was always there.

We made a pilgrimage to our shrine of Our Lady of Sorrows on her feast day, September 15. It began with a cake, which a number of singing women carried into the dining room. It was a blue cake with icing, decorated with a small statue of the Madonna, a beautiful red heart and seven burning tapers, which represented the swords that pierced her heart.

We stood, later that evening, praying the Sorrowful Mysteries of the Rosary before the statue of Our Lady of Sorrows. I looked a long time at Our Lady. She stands forlorn, tears on her cheeks, hands clasped in an attitude of exquisite agony, a poignant and haunting figure of sorrow. Our Lady grips the heart and mind. She is hard to look away from.

She was the most privileged lady God ever made, conceived without sin. God the Holy Spirit placed into the chalice of her slim body the divinity of God the Son and she gave birth to him!

She became the Mother of God. Her womb was his heaven on earth. She fed him, the Almighty, with the milk of her body. She caressed and kissed him. What other human being ever held God in her arms and kissed him?

But oh, poor lady, poor lady! Life was a long tragedy for her. For she knew that he came to be a holocaust.

He must be tortured and killed and offered up to God for the sake of humanity. She, poor lady, must offer him up as his Father did.

She must not interfere with the bloody sacrifice. In fact, she must do all she can to see that the sacrifice is completed; and she must love all those who torture him and kill him, for they are her children. Yes, even they.

His Father is the Father of all men and women. His mother must be the mother of all men and women.

She was essential to the redemption of all humanity, because her will was one with God's will. She obeyed God, through love, as completely as a rudder obeys the slightest wish of the hand that guides it.

She said to the angel Gabriel, "Behold the handmaid of the Lord, be it done to me according to thy word" (Lk 1:38).

The Child was born and grew up to change the world and to die on the cross.

She stood for three hours beneath his cross. She watched him suffer. She watched him die.

The cross held the wonder of the Body of the living God. It was saturated with his Blood. But, despite the agony, there was peace in that cross. And solace. And healing. And infinite power.

God's will was being done. The slaves of sin were being freed. She saw the price of redemption as it was paid.

Christ died there, on that cross. But in his death, he triumphed over the world, and the flesh, and the devil. He had done his Father's will. He had redeemed all men and women, all Mary's children. He opened heaven to them. Had Mary not known joy as well as desolation at the foot of the cross, I think she would have died. There was great sadness in her heart but also great joy and triumph.

Staying in the Word of God

St. Jerome
September 30

"Heaven and earth will pass away, but my words will never pass away." (Mt 24:35)

There is a permanence about that sentence that we don't quite understand, because in our experience, everything changes. We go so quickly from sickness to health. We're low one day and high the next. We're rich and we're poor. Everything changes. We change our jobs, we change our ideas. What we're really looking for is permanence.

We're really looking for security of some kind, but the only real security is in God. We need him all the time because we are human and weak; we are still children. We're always tempted to have our own way no matter what, and how often we walk into dangers without seeing them!

Any one of us is a potential murderer. Any one of us is so unstable that we could fall into a rage and kill somebody. It has happened to the gentlest of people. A sudden rage erupts in us that we can't explain.

Yes, many, many things happen to us that surprise us, so unstable are we. We pick up a purse with money in it and we are tempted to keep it. "Finders keepers, losers weepers." We may even know to whom it belongs, but we're going to keep it anyway. We won't even have to mention it on our income tax! We say, "Such temptations are only human." Yes, human according to our corrupt nature. We're unstable. We want what we want, when we want it. And we all want very much!

Yet, if we stopped and thought about God and his unchanging word, he would help us. If we listened to Our Lord in the Gospel, we wouldn't think that maybe God sent this money to me for some reason! We would know such thinking was stupid and a rationalization. Somebody lost it, period! Wherever we go, whatever we do, we will always be tempted to do our own will and not the will of God.

We simply forget that everything passes. The money that we found will be quickly spent. Whatever it bought will be quickly destroyed.

Nothing lasts except God, his word and his love. If we stay with him, his word will keep our minds and hearts in the words and actions and love of Jesus Christ. Then we can't go wrong. If we don't remain in his love and in his Word, we certainly will go wrong.

October

A Rosebud and a Return
St. Thérèse of the Child Jesus
October 1

In 1935 I was assigned by *Liberty Magazine* to interview Father Charles Coughlin, the famous radio priest in Detroit, who was at the Shrine of Saint Thérèse of Lisieux, the Little Flower.

He refused to see me. I had $2,500 to give him for an interview, but it didn't mean anything. I was America's star reporter. I was highly paid. I wasn't supposed to flop. My editor was not pleased. He said, "What the hell kind of a reporter are you? You're supposed to be the world's greatest and you can't even crack a little country priest." So I was determined to get into the Shrine of the Little Flower and to make her priest say something.

Days and days passed and I got nowhere near the shrine. I whiled away the time by reading Father Coughlin's views on social justice and in digging up bits out of his life. And I got to wondering about his patroness, St. Thérèse, the Little Flower. She had done great things for him, but I knew nothing about her. I went to a book store and bought *The Story of a Soul: The Autobiography of the Little Flower*.

That night, lying in bed in a room at the Book Cadillac Hotel, I took up her story, yawned, and began to read. I intended merely to glance through it, but once I started to read those enchanted pages I could not put the book aside. Even after I had finished them, at three o'clock in the morning, I must have held

Getting to Know God

the book in my hands for an hour or more, and rubbed tear-wet fingers over its covers. No book has ever stirred me, as did that simple, beautiful story written by a girl in her twenties, a nun shivering in her cold little cell as she wrote.

If I could write like that! Ah yes! And if I could live like that!

Once I too had known the love of God. I had played priest at an improvised altar when I was a child. I had been an altar boy. I too had wanted to become a saint. I had fought to enter a monastery at the age of thirteen. I remembered the serenity of the monastery as I lay propped against the pillows. I could see the statue of the Blessed Virgin Mary in the Chapel, the jewels hung on her by pious lay people, the glory of her face. I could hear again the rhythmic chant of the monks. It had been thirty years or so since I had worn the black tunic and scapular of the Servites, with the big wooden rosary dangling from my belt—yet, for a little while, I was a monk again, a postulant waiting impatiently to become a novice.

What had happened?

I had left the monastery. I didn't regret that. And I had become a newspaperman. I didn't regret that either. And I had become the great Eddie Doherty, fat-head, free-thinker, and amateur rake. That I did regret, and bitterly. I don't mean I was "converted" then and there, or that I determined immediately to return to my Father's house. I merely began to realize some of the things I had lost—the clean joy of loving God and of striving to know his will, and doing it; the wonder of a clean conscience; the hope of attaining heaven; the glory of complete and child-like trust in God; the bliss to be found in renunciation.

And I remembered other things—the self-pity and horror I discovered when I knelt at my father's coffin and realized I was unworthy so much as to pronounce the name of God even in secret—the despair that flooded me when I tried to pray for my son Jack—and then the taste of dust and ashes in my mouth when I tried to thank him, that day when I saw my son, who had been crippled with infantile paralysis, walk without a brace.

I tried to make myself believe the tears in my eyes were born of the beauty of the book I had just finished. I tried to make myself believe they were not over the regret of my misspent years or determination to change my ways. But I had seen a light, and in that light I had caught a glimpse of myself. That's why I was weeping.

I realized that the lovely saint had thrown me one of her roses, that I had wet it with my tears, and that it would grow—but I didn't want to realize it. Not yet. I felt I wasn't ready to go back to the Church. It was too big a thing to seize immediately, this heaven-sent impulse. I had been away too long. I had lost the faith. It would be hypocritical to return now. Let Sister Thérèse's rose grow, if it would take root in such sour soil. If it brought forth other flowers someday, well, I wouldn't be the gardener.

Someday, I finally conceded, maybe I would go back to the Church. But not right away.

Daylight was streaming through the window before the spell of the Little Flower left me, and I remembered I had a difficult assignment in Detroit.

"Listen, Little Flower," I said, "you wanted to spend your life in heaven doing good for those on earth, sending down showers of roses. Throw me a little bud, will you? Let me see this tough priest who won't see any reporter. Give me half a break and I'll make him talk."

On my way to breakfast, I met an old friend, with whom I'd worked on Chicago newspapers twenty years before. When he heard I hadn't seen Father Coughlin, he called a friend of his who got me in to see the famous priest within the hour!

Father Coughlin greeted me cordially enough, but he was still stubborn about giving me a story. "You thought it would be easy to see a Catholic priest, didn't you?" he charged. "Just because you are a Catholic!"

It was then I told him I had left the Church. It was then we discussed the religion I had adopted as my own—a trust in God so simple I could do anything I pleased and get away with it. I don't think the priest could have been shocked more if I had zipped a spit-ball at him. Nor more annoyed with me. It was then he dealt me that punch below the belt, asking, "But can God trust you?"

"I'll tell you what we'll do," he said, after his anger had worn thin. "If you promise to go to Confession and Communion, and to go to Mass every Sunday for the rest of your life, I'll give you a story. I never gave anybody a story, but I'll give you one."

I pretended indignation.

"What? You want me to sell my soul for a story?"

"No soul, no story."

"Sold!"

We shook hands on the bargain, and he walked up and down, and the brogue came on him, and he dictated a story. I wrote it, adding to it all the material I had collected before the interview. My editor wired me a bouquet of pretty words and advertised my soul extensively in promoting the story. My soul was probably the best advertised in all the world.

My wife Mildred was waiting for me when I returned to New York after interviewing Father Coughlin. She was troubled over a dream she'd had. She had faith in dreams. She explained the gist of the dream to me. "Eddie, you must go back to the Church," she said.

It was then I told her about my bargain with Father Coughlin.

I kept my part of the bargain, so far as I could. I went to Confession, but I could not get absolution and I could not go to Communion because I had not been married in the Church. I was still "outside the pale." I had duties and responsibilities, but no privileges and no rights.

I went to Mass every Sunday, though at first I felt ridiculous and somewhat hypocritical. There was no particular feeling of fervor in me. I was going to church not to honor God, but to keep a word I had given—to pay on the instalment plan, as it were, for the story of Father Coughlin. But gradually the feeling changed. Old prayers came back to me, sweet-tasting on my lips. Old hymns sang themselves again to me, in Latin and in English. And the time came when I wanted most desperately to receive communion and return completely to my Father's house, but could not. So long as I put off marrying as a Catholic, I must remain thus outside the walls. I could not even peek into the garden where I knew he walked. Yet I kept remembering the tactless priest who, when Mildred and I had approached him to be married, had told us that we were living in sin. I was not going to let any priest tell us that again.

Mildred accompanied me to church every Sunday. She was intrigued by the Church. Eventually she wanted to become a Catholic. But before she could, she was killed in a freak accident while we were visiting California.

She went out alone one day for a walk in the mountains. She didn't return. Later, after the police recovered her body, I learned what had happened. She fell eight feet down a mountain gully. She hit her head against a stone or something hard. It knocked her out, the deputy said. Her throat was jammed against three little branches of a mesquite tree. She choked to death while she was unconscious.

A priest came to see me after the sheriff had gone. He asked quite a few questions about Mildred and I told him about her. I told him she had wanted to become a Catholic.

"There are three kinds of baptism, you know," the priest said gently. "There is baptism of water, baptism of blood, and baptism of desire. Your wife was baptized, and, I'm sure, went straight to heaven. The Good Shepherd was walking the hills yesterday when she fell. And he's taken her home in his arms."

We took Mildred to Chicago, my two boys and I, and left her there in hallowed ground. In a few days we returned to New York. There, on a quiet side street, I found a little church, and, in a darkened corner of it, a priest waiting to hear my sins and give me absolution.

How long had he been waiting there for me? Who can say? How long had that little mesquite bush been growing on that hill in California? It seemed to me, kneeling in the shadows outside the confessional, that God had planted that bush for Mildred as surely as he had placed this priest for me; and that he had made his plans for her and for me eons before we met.

I had deserted God. I had hoped to forget him. I had defied and flouted him. I had denied him. I had tried to hate him. And yet, there was his minister, his agent, his chosen representative, waiting to forgive me, in his name, for all that I had done and all that I had culpably left undone, waiting to take me back into the Church and make me once more a child of God.

After I had made my confession, it seemed that Mildred was outside the confessional, saying "Didn't I tell you something wonderful was going to happen to you? Didn't I, Eddie? Wasn't I right?" It seemed to me that the Little Flower was somewhere around too, rejoicing. We are told that there is great joy in heaven over the repentance of a sinner. Let me say there is great joy on earth as well—as great a joy as this particular sinner has ever known.

Autumn Glory Days

The air is black and blue with birds. The blue jays scream and the black crows caw. I thought the jays had chased the crows out of this bailiwick, but I could have been wrong. Mists rise from the water. The pumpkin by the pigpen puts on weight—like the pigs that watch it greedily—and yearns for the frost that will give it a Halloween beauty.

A few fishermen still are here in Ontario, but most of them have gone back to Ohio and Pennsylvania and Indiana and New York, to tell fish stories through the winter.

One angler tells of a giant pike he almost caught. The monster was brought to the side of the boat after a terrific struggle. Then he leaped up, bit the line in two, and swam away.

Another follower of St. Peter swears the same fish—or one even perhaps a little bigger—came into view just as a nice fat pickerel was readying for the gaff. He swallowed the pickerel and ran.

The trees are turning color, each trying to outshine the other in her autumn outfit. The wind has a tang we have not felt since April. The mornings are chill. October has come—to remind us that all things change and all things die.

Yet in the memory of a man gazing at the slate-gray river and the gray-blue sky, there are many things that do not change or need any frost to give them beauty. In his memory are the faces of young men and women who came to Madonna House in the past few years to live with us a time, to work, to play, to ask questions, to pray, to study, and to get the feel of the Catholic lay apostolate.

They did a thousand different jobs for us. They helped cut the hay and hoist the bales into our barn. They dug the earth and mixed it with manure. They planted. They "unplanted"—especially the potatoes. They helped with our monthly newspaper, *Restoration*. They picked berries and apples, rhubarb and peas. They canned. They washed and scrubbed. They filed. They typed. They helped to cook the noon and evening meals. They worked!

The memory nothing will kill is the memory of them as they sat on the veranda or in the dining room in the evening and talked of God and the Church. There was such hunger in them, such eagerness to learn about their Catholic faith. They soaked up everything Catherine and the priests could present for their consideration.

One boy especially shines in this memory, a boy not yet twenty. He was working his way through a Catholic college. It had been his custom to hire out for the summer vacations, to work as a waiter in a swank resort or a clerk in a big city bank—anything that would pay him decently. He gave us his entire vacation—not for pay, but for what he could find out about his religion.

He wanted to be more than the average Catholic. He wanted to do something for God but didn't know what to do. He said he felt more than repaid for his work by learning that one must "be" before he "does," that one must be a lover of God before he works for God, that one must *be* a real Catholic before he attempts any kind of Catholic Action.

He hitchhiked home toward the beginning of September, his face shining in the morning sun, much as it used to shine in the soft evening light. He had found his vocation in Madonna House, he said. He was going to be a priest.

I couldn't tell you how many young faces there are in my memories. I can tell you only that they are the faces of people who want to be saints, and they are all beautiful.

Combermere is one of the most beautiful regions on earth. It is lovely even on a gray, chill day. But the young men and the young women who come here give it an added beauty, give it a luster that approaches the supernatural.

It's good to live with saints, even novice saints. It's difficult, though, at times to realize these kids possess such unusual sanctity; they're so full of laughter, and they're ignorant of so many things. Thank God Madonna House attracts them.

Let the leaves fall, dying in their autumn glory. Let the calm surface of the river roughen. Let the winter come. Let the winds howl, if they will. In the sitting room of Madonna House, in the twilight or the velvet dark of night, after night prayers, there will always be a touch of eager, jealous, God-hungry spring.

Listening to God
Our Lady of the Rosary
October 7

It seems so simple, to listen to God all the time. Yet, it's probably the most difficult thing to do. There are so many distractions—people who need us, or hate us, or want us to do something for them.

People eat us up with their own problems, with their own agonies, with their own demands, and sometimes even with their own joys. Did you ever know of anybody who, on returning from a big trip somewhere, just couldn't stop telling you all about it?

We can't possibly think of God all the time, because of the pressure of people around us. And yet, if we make the sincere intention of living every moment for God, with God, and in God, we won't bother about anything else. It won't matter if we don't think of God for hours at a time. The fact that we want to, the fact that we have made this intention, this desire of wanting to hear God all the time, is somehow enough, as far as God is concerned.

It's like you go to bed with a rosary in your hands. You want to pray it with love for Our Lady and Our Lord, but you fall asleep. That's nature overcoming you. Don't worry about it. There's a legend that Our Lady and the angels will finish it for you. You had the intention of saying it, so don't worry about it.

It's that way with the voice of Christ. Sometimes you don't hear it; you're wrapped up in something else. You're rushing somebody to the hospital, let's say. You can't think of God or anything else. You're thinking of the person you're taking to the hospital, what's going to happen to him or her. Subconsciously in your mind you may be saying a little prayer, but your actual attention is all on the person you are loving by helping take them to the hospital.

When we're all wrapped up in the work we are doing, we don't explicitly think of God; we think of what we're doing, and how to do it well. The fact that God is in your heart makes everything you do a prayer. Your concern for this person in the ambulance, for instance, is a prayer, a great prayer, because it's an unselfish act. It comes out of your own heart. It's love at its best. It's a prayer because love is prayer.

Seeing God's Glory

It was an October day. The flaming crimson of the maples had almost left the woods, but there was still magnificence in God's world. Great patches of russet and rust and mustard and gold and green! Green of the eternal hills. Green of eternal hope, and love and mercy, and divine assurance.

I saw October falling apart that day, so close to my eighty-first birthday; and I saw myself standing like an empty tree, holding my arms up to the God of heaven and earth, trying to explain why I had no more golden leaves to sacrifice for him.

I had come back to Combermere from a visit to my seeing-eye doctor in Toronto. He had promised that within a few weeks of my cataract surgery I would have almost perfect vision in my right eye. I returned with a temporary pair of glasses.

And I could see!

I had never been blind, but there had been times when I saw as through a veil. Coming home from Toronto, I saw all things with new eyes.

I thought of the Bible story of the man born blind, whom Jesus healed (Jn 9:1-38). When he looked up after the Savior had spoken, he saw the full glory of God shining on him out of the eyes of a Man. Who can even try to describe his emotions! How can I describe what I felt when I saw the glory of God shining on me in those October red maple mosaics!

The world is new again. And I am new. At eighty-one, I am brand new! And new thoughts keep coming into my old mind.

I thought of the cross on Golgotha and saw the good thief talking to the dying Son of God. "Remember me when you come into your kingdom," he said to Jesus. This is the essence of what we now call "the Jesus prayer"—"Lord Jesus, have mercy on me, a sinner."

"This day," Jesus answered, "you will be with me in paradise" (Lk 23:42-43).

The man born blind saw the glory of God. The good thief dying in agony saw the mercy of God shining in those glorious eyes! He must have thought his crucifixion a blessing he did not deserve.

I would give not only my right eye but the left one and all the rest of me, to see what that most fortunate of all thieves—of all sinners—saw in his last few moments. Even before he died, he was in paradise!

In a few seconds, in a few words, a man wipes out an entire life of crime. In a few seconds, in a few words, a roughneck and repulsive sinner becomes a saint to be envied by all the world.

I remember, crazily enough, an old-time ad: "Don't envy that school girl complexion; have one of your own."

Don't envy the good thief's sudden conversion and quick entry into heaven. Have one of your own.

Would it seem absurd if I said that Mary, the Blessed Mother, had prayed for this momentous happening and that she never prays in vain? She wanted to give both thieves a free one-way trip to heaven. And she wanted to give her Son two saints to accompany him on his journey home. The grace was offered to both thugs. They could take it or reject it. It was a superb gift. But neither God nor his mother ever interferes with the free will of a human being.

Jesus was giving supreme gifts too. He gave his life to his Father for us. He gave his mother to John, the Beloved Apostle—"This is your mother"—and through John, to us. And he gave John to her—"Woman, this is your son"—John and all the rest of us (Jn 19:26-27).

On Calvary Jesus wove a red carpet of his blood to welcome sinners home. Here on earth we give "the red carpet treatment" to VIPs, but to God, everybody who asks for mercy, even the bum dying in the dirt of the street, is a VIP. It doesn't matter how dirty his shoes. The carpet is unrolled for him with great joy, and with all the angels singing.

November

Ask For Help

All Saints Day
November 1

At one time in my life, if anybody had asked me what my ambition was, I would have answered, "I'm going to be a saint, or go to hell trying."

Of course nobody goes to hell trying to be a saint; but I wasn't too sure about that then. I wasn't too sure what a saint was. I guess I thought it was a simple "do it yourself" proposition. You let God help you, but you also had to help him, and do most of the work.

Only a sinner can praise God on earth. Only a saint can praise him in heaven. One has to be a saint to enter heaven, but a sinner can be a saint if he asks for help. Some sinners do and some don't.

I didn't always ask help from the saints. After all, I was a newspaperman. I could take care of myself.

Now I know better. I need the help of the saints and I ask for it, especially from my favorites, like St. Thérèse the Little Flower and St. Martin de Porres. And of course, Our Lady.

* * *

After my ordination, one of my grandsons wrote me, "First step, the priesthood, second step, sanctity."

Sanctity! I must become a saint!

But how? By wearing a hair shirt? That is good for some people. Not for me. By scourging myself? Oh no! Anybody but me! By fasting? My doctors and nurses won't let me. By rubbing cigarette stubs in my food or using nauseating ingredients? Unthinkable! Who can spoil any food while so many millions of people starve?

Jesus fasted, but only for those forty days and nights. We never heard that he spoiled his food, wore hair shirts, whipped himself or did anything like that in the way of atonement. We do know that he accepted joyfully whatever indignity, humiliation, rejection, or suffering his Father willed him to suffer. We know also that he died the death his Father wanted him to die. So it occurred to me to follow him in this—to accept, with such love and gratitude as I can, all the penances the Most High wishes me to suffer for his sake.

Death

All Souls Day
November 2

October died a couple of days ago. It passed away quietly in its sleep and its crib was given to November. Today the snow is falling and people are praying for the souls in purgatory. It is the month to pray for the souls of those departed.

Death is a natural thing. But it's also natural that we don't want to die—at least right now. Even the saints don't want to die too soon, no matter how eager they may be to climb God's holy mountain. Death is inevitable, of course. We shall all die. I will die and so will you. Everybody around us and about us has died, is dying or will die. God made death so that he could give us eternal life. Only through dying can anyone get to heaven. Only by dying can anyone attain undying joy.

Priests, especially our Madonna House priests, bless every graveyard they pass by. One of them hails the dead in words of joy. "Keep shining in glory, you lucky children of the Lord!"

Favors from Martin

St. Martin de Porres
November 3

The best way to get acquainted with St. Martin de Porres is to ask a favor of him.

It is important to get acquainted with St. Martin, if one does not already know him. For it is important to get acquainted with God, and Martin leads his friends to Mary, and through her, to her Son.

Martin de Porres was born in Lima, Peru in 1579, the illegitimate son of a white man—a proud Spaniard—and a black woman whose people had been slaves. Because he looked more like his mother in color and in features, many white people despised and distrusted him. His father deserted them and Martin grew up in poverty.

Now and then, Martin's father sent a few gold pieces to Lima, but not often, apparently, and not very many. It is recorded that Martin sometimes got into trouble because of those yellow coins.

His mother would send him out to buy food. Sometimes he met people poorer than himself and gave them the money. Sometimes he bought the food he was sent for, but gave it to people hungrier than himself. His mother punished him, but never could break him of the habit of giving away whatever he had to give.

Martin was baptized, learned to read and write, and was later confirmed. Between the ages of ten and twelve, he was thrown more or less on his own resources for a living. Unloved by his mother, abandoned by his father, he lived in neglect, loneliness and poverty.

The boy often visited Lima's magnificent churches, which were cool and peaceful. It was in one of these churches that Martin de Porres found out that God loved him and that Christ had died for him and had established the Church for him, and all the sacraments.

Martin read books when he could get them, books about Christ and Mary and the saints. But it was the crucifix that was Martin's best book. In the silence of the nights, Martin studied the books and the crucifix. In the silence of Our Lady, Martin laid the foundation for that love of God that overflowed into love not only for all men and women, but even for animals, even such insignificant creatures as mice.

Martin became apprenticed to a barber-surgeon. He learned not only how to cut hair and trim mustaches, but also how to set bones, tend wounds, dose fevers, and compound various herbs as medicines for various diseases. To what he was taught, he added the medicine of unselfish love. Martin knew that love could cure, sometimes, when all other remedies had failed.

Lima began to take note of the boy. He was always smiling, and his touch evicted pain and healed. Strange things happened. A man with a raging fever sipped a little water Martin handed him, and was cured within the hour. Another, stabbed in a dozen places, saw the boy sprinkle a little powder on him. He watched his wounds close. He walked away, wondering. An old woman came to Martin with a migraine. She went skipping home with a basket of food on her arm. Babies looked at him and smiled, and even the most desperately sick among them responded quickly to his caress on their foreheads.

Eventually, Martin became a Dominican lay brother and lived in the convent of the Most Holy Rosary, serving all the servants of God. There are many stories of Martin's sanctity and the miracles God performed through him.

One centered about a patient in the convent, Brother Francisco Velasco, who was dying of dropsy. He had been placed in an isolated room in the novitiate and the doors were locked and bolted at the hour stipulated in the rules. He was alone. He was in pain. He was burning with thirst, for the doctor had given orders he was not to have any water. It was wretchedly cold. The novitiate was not heated, and the night was bitter.

Suddenly Martin was there, looking down at him with a friendly smile. His arms were laden with linen and sweet-smelling rosemary, and he held a pan full of red-hot coals.

Immediately, Brother Francisco began to feel warm and good. He no longer felt any pain. He no longer felt any thirst. Martin washed the novice, put a clean linen tunic on him, changed the sheets on his bed and sprinkled them with the rosemary leaves. Then he told the patient to go to sleep.

"You are not going to die," he reassured the young man. "You will be much better when you awake."

The novice could not help asking questions.

"How did you know I needed you so? How do you know I am not going to die? Do you know more than the doctor? And how did you get in here? The doors are locked and bolted. Have you a key?"

Martin answered only with a smile. The boy turned his head for a moment, and when he turned back to ask another question, Martin was not there. He had disappeared as mysteriously as he had come.

The novice tried to figure it out, but he fell asleep. Perhaps it was nothing but a dream, he thought in the morning. He stretched his arms and started to get up. He recollected himself. He was a dying man. Then he realized he was no such thing. He was more alive than he had been before. He was so full of life he wanted to jump out of bed and hurry to the chapel to thank God! But, he remembered, the doors were locked. He must wait.

The doctor came early that morning, with the novice master. He didn't believe what he saw. The patient was entirely cured. There was not the least sign of dropsy in him. What is more, he was absurdly healthy and ravenously hungry, and bothered about only one thing—how did Martin get into his room last night?

The novice master, Father Andres de Lizon, asserted again and again that both the first and second doors had been securely locked. He had the keys in his possession. Nobody else had had them, for even a fraction of a second, during the night.

He was not as surprised as the others, however, to learn that Martin had apparently gone through the walls with his vessel of burning coals, as though he were a spirit, and the glowing embers and the linens and the herbs were spirits too. He had witnessed this phenomenon several times before. Many other rooms had been locked and bolted; but Martin had appeared in them suddenly, smiling, eager to help, and laden with all the things he needed—just as Christ had appeared to the apostles when they were together after the Resurrection.

Father de Lizon could have told the doctor and the novice many other tales of Martin; but he did not. He kept them to himself until the right time came, when he was called before the Church court to testify in the process of Martin's canonization.

After Martin's death, these and many other witnesses came forward and told their stories before the Church tribunals, giving their testimony to the sanctity of Brother Martin de Porres. He was humble. He was charitable. He was devoted to the Virgin Mother of God. He was ever at work. He was obedient to his superiors. He fed the poor. He healed the sick. He was found in rapture, seen high up in the chapel, suspended in air, before a crucifix.

Every mouth opened in Martin's behalf tells of his holiness; and, if it speaks of miracles, it does so casually, almost as an afterthought. It was wonderful that a mere man could be so holy; it was not wonderful at all that a holy man could work miracles. Even today, friends of Martin bear witness to his holiness—and the wonders his holiness has wrought.

Martin de Porres died in Lima, Peru on November 3, 1639. Of the many, many miracles after his death, two were "juridically proved" by Church authorities before Pope Gregory XVI declared Martin a blessed servant of God.

Elvira Mariano, of Lima, had her right eyeball cut out by a piece of pottery—a vase broke as she was taking it down from a window ledge. Don Pedro de Urdanibia, then the most eminent physician in Lima, was called.

"The eye," he said, "is entirely gone. Only God can give you a new one."

A Dominican friar applied a relic, a tiny piece of one of Martin's bones, to her eye. Immediately Elvira felt a "soothing influence" in the empty eye-socket. She slept for an hour, and thought the wound had healed. She slept again, until morning, when she found she had been given a new eye.

The second miracle concerned the fall of a two-year-old child, Melchior Varanda, from the window of his mother's house to the pavement some twenty feet below. His skull was crushed. The same celebrated surgeon who attended Señora Mariano told the boy's mother that the only doctor who could help the child was Brother Martin. A neighbor drew a rude portrait of Martin and pressed it against the child's bleeding head with a prayer.

In less than three hours, say the witnesses, the boy was running around the house in his usual fashion—without any sign of injury and no visible symptom of shock.

Many people insist even today that God is working miracles through Martin's intercession for those who implore his aid. It is significant that in this most unbelieving time, more and more people should turn so confidently for help and comfort to a miracle-worker who died more than three hundred years ago. It is significant that in this time of bigotry and intolerance, they call upon the spirit of a man of mixed races for their necessities. It is significant that in this time of pride and materialism, multitudes should pay fealty to a humble Dominican lay brother who never had or wanted anything for himself.

How can you lose, asking help of Martin? He can still accomplish wonders and it is never too late to ask a favor of him, or a miracle. But it is best to do it now!

Personal Favors: From New Jersey to Harlem

I became acquainted with St. Martin de Porres when I was asked to do an article about him for *Liberty Magazine*. The Dominicans in New York City gave me information on him and I wrote a piece called "Hurrying Heaven." He was Blessed Martin at the time and people wanted to get the last miracle required by the Church before he could be canonized a saint. They wanted to hurry up the process.

A woman in New Jersey read my story and she called up to tell me there was a little boy with a terrible lung problem and would I go see him with a relic of Blessed Martin to cure this boy. She had great faith!

So Father Norbert Georges, a Dominican, and I went in my car out to St. Francis Hospital in Trenton. We learned this little boy had lost a whole lung. He had ruptured it in a furious crying fit. The X-rays showed that. His case was so rare that the greatest specialists in Trenton, Camden and Philadelphia came to see him and study him. Dozens of X-rays showed the lung was shattered beyond repair.

The boy was in a little oxygen tent. You could hear him wheezing all the way down the corridor. As you came close to him, you could hear wheezing, wheezing, wheezing. It went through your nerves. We came into his room and saw a little wasted figure. He looked like a wax doll. You wouldn't give two cents for his life. He was breathing through hollow needles. They were stuck into his chest on both sides. He couldn't breath the air out. The air collected in the pleural cavity and its only outlet was through those hollow needles and that's what caused the wheezing.

Father Georges pinned the second class relic of Martin to the boy's nightgown, took my relic of Martin and blessed him with it, and let his mother kiss the relic. He prayed silently and told the mother not to worry any longer. Then we went away.

In six days, the X-rays showed the boy had a new lung! The doctors said, "We don't believe it. Lungs don't just repair themselves. This is a new lung—there's no repair; it's a new lung! The X-rays show it, they prove it. Nothing we did can mean anything. This is an outstanding miracle."

So I wrote another story on Martin, this time about the miracle.

I really got attached to Martin. He does a lot of things for me. Incredible things!

One of the best things was what Martin did for me while I was doing another story for *Liberty Magazine*. It was an article on the city of Harlem. We were going to call it "The Wickedest City in the World." An old friend found out I was doing the story and insisted I go interview a Russian baroness who was working with the poor in a place called Friendship House. This baroness was living in Harlem and working with both blacks and whites. This was long before the Civil Rights movement.

Another reporter and I went to her apartment, but nobody was there. Then, going down 135th Street, I saw the Friendship House storefront, and also a sign for the de Porres Catholic Lending Library. We went in.

The first thing I noticed was the peace in the place. Harlem is a big, bustling, noisy city, full of unrest and agitation. But here was a very peaceful atmosphere, with boys and girls, black and white. People were singing, talking, reading. And there was this good-looking blond over in the corner. It was the Baroness.

She sat at a desk, writing, smoking a cigarette. A statue of Blessed Martin was in a niche behind her, a vigil light burning in a red glass at its feet. I winked, glad to see it. It did not wink back.

The Baroness had ink on her fingers. Her pen leaked. The elbow of her ragged blue sweater had a hole in it. I had heard she was a saint. So what? She was a blond. Her eyes were blue, with stars or sapphires, or bonfires in them. She wasn't the sort of beauty I was accustomed to look at, and to take out to lunch or dinner. She had a beauty I had never seen before, a beauty that grew and intensified as I watched it. Maybe it was the beauty of a saint.

She looked up, saw us, smiled, and very graciously greeted us. I said, "I'm Eddie Doherty from *Liberty Magazine*," and she said, "*Liberty Magazine*—we don't allow that dirty rag in here. You can't peddle that here, Mister."

I said, "I'm not trying to peddle it, Baroness. I'm here because you're supposed to be the authority on Harlem. We're writing a story on Harlem, the wickedest city in the world."

Well, she bristled. That was good, because it's good to get a woman mad, because then she talks, talks her head off if she's mad enough.

Before she could throw us out, we sat down and looked very meek and mild and let her orate, which she proceeded to do. She told me what she thought of the rest of New York, which made Harlem a victim. I looked at the statue of Martin and wondered whether this guy was bringing us together, and why? I wondered why he was there and what this woman knew about Martin. So when she was through with her harangue, I pointed to the statue and said, "Is that a Negro saint there?" as if I didn't know anything about him at all.

And she said, "Well, I don't know whether you're Catholic or what you are, but you asked me about him and I'm going to tell you." So she started telling me about Martin! She went into the story of his life and midway, she said, "He was always in Lima." That was my opening. So I said, "He wasn't always in Lima." And she said, "What do you mean, he wasn't always in Lima?" I said, "Well, he spent two years in Ecuador." And then she said, "So you knew about him all the time!" I said, "I probably know more about him than you ever will!"

Then I wrote her a check and she asked, "Will it bounce?" I said, "No, it won't come back, but I will." And that was the way I met Catherine, how the whole thing started. And Martin was there, right in the middle of it.

* * *

November is a restless month. It hurries, hurries, hurries, shortening its days as it rushes on. It is eager to get out of the way so that the world can be blessed again with Christmas.

December

Canadian Winter

People still ask, "Are you going to spend the entire winter up there in Canada?" And they still ask, "How can you stand it?"

We usually deprecate the heroism imputed to us in our determination to remain in Combermere with some such silly remark as "It never gets colder here than fifty below zero," or "There is seldom more than six feet of snow—except, of course, in the drifts."

The truth is that we love the winter. Winter, like death, is not at all terrible when one prepares for it. And we are well prepared.

There is, for instance, plenty of fuel. Our shed is filled with cord wood. Birch, elm and maple, with here and there a little pine.

The storm windows are on. The garden produce from summer has been put into jars that line our cellar shelves. The bees have been made snug and their honey will last us until the flowers bloom again. Our hay is in.

Heavy coats and socks and shoes have been taken down from the attic and the light summer stuff has been put away. The boats have been taken from the water and stored in a dry place.

The chimney flues have been cleaned and snow shovels are in the garage, ready to cut wide, neat paths.

I shall be called upon, I know, to see that somebody shovels snow wherever needed; and I am ready to do so. Always ready to watch somebody work—that's me! Of course, if it weren't for my enlarged and sclerosed aorta, I'd help in other ways. Natch!

The point is, with me or without me, all things go along smoothly at Madonna House, preparing for Advent, for the birthday of the Little Stranger, for the New Year, for the winter months.

With my help, or without it, I get older every day, come nearer and nearer to my last Advent. I don't think I am at all prepared for that; but I should like to be. The doctor in Chicago gave me thirty-five years more.

But suppose he was merely being optimistic! What if I have only thirty years left, and not thirty-five? How can I adequately prepare myself in that time against the winter that will claim me? Of course I have people here to help me—but even so, it's going to be tough! I will have to do some of the work myself, I know!

You will tell me, perhaps, that the Little Flower did a pretty good job of getting ready in much less than thirty years. You will, of course, cite the example of the good thief on the cross who did it in thirty seconds.

But I am neither the good nun nor the good thief. I must go my own way, make my preparations in my own muddled fashion, and take my chances on God's mercy. Even as you, my friend—even as you yourself!

Still, as we say here in Combermere, God's justice never goes fifty degrees below his mercy—and only your own drifts ever bury you from the sight and the warmth of his love.

And that celestial winter—Boy!—they say it's more wonderful than life. I hope we're both all set.

———

An Advent Amethyst
First Day of Winter
December 21

Dear God, Loving Father of Us All,

The snow falls softly today. The flakes dance and whirl. They flutter and hesitate, as they near the earth, trying to pick out a likely place to land. Then they drift to it, or as close to it as the boorish wind will let them.

The snowflakes speak of God, of moisture seeping into the soil to kiss to life the seeds in spring. The snowflakes speak of the Immaculate Mary, and of the graces that sift down to us through her holy hands.

Children play in the snow, like saints in Mary's graces. People ride through the powdery nights, to sing to neighbors about the little town of Bethlehem and the Child laid in a manger. People invite them in for steaming cups of tea or coffee. People sometimes sing carols with them.

This morning, Lord, by your grace, I shuffled a short way up the road, taking it easy, my mukluks making the first tracks in your nice, new fall of snow. I was a fugitive from a cyclone of Christmas preparations. My room swarmed with girls cleaning and dusting and scrubbing.

I sauntered down to the kitchen, and there were girls besieging a gigantic turkey and several hams with fearful, shiny weapons. Girls were icing cookies—Christmas trees and wise men, the baby Christ and legions of fat angels.

Even the chapel, where the boys were painting the floor, was out of bounds.

Outside the snow was light, invigorating. The wind was man-sized, but the day wasn't really cold. Let it be recorded that December 21 was a pleasant sort of day. You kept sifting your flakes upon me, Lord, like a storm of blessings. You kept fanning the wind in my direction. It caressed me. It whispered of you. It smelled of heaven—and of pine. I kept trudging on, thinking about the way we prepare for Christmas.

We make a fuss about it; and we want the whole, hostile world to feel deeply about it. It is an effort, in our day "to keep Christ in Christmas." Some of us seem to think we are doing you a favor in celebrating the birthday of your Son. We forget that you give us infinitely more each morning in the Mass than we can ever repay. We forget that, in the Mass, you do not simply hand us the Baby, as Mary did when she put him into the arms of Simeon the prophet. You fill us with him. Every day, really, is Christmas day to us!

The snow stopped. So did the wind. And so did I. And at that moment, the sun, which had been skulking, sent the gray clouds sprawling out of its impatient path, and showed me a world of radiance and glory!

The hieroglyphics my feet had carved into the snow sparkled and gleamed and glittered. The road turned into a lane of powdered amethysts and sapphires and emeralds and diamonds. The evergreens stood out boldly in the glare, their ruffles trimmed with ermine. These were the candy-sprinkled Christmas tree cookies of our kitchen, transformed and brought to life. And over them floated the snow-white, shining clouds, the banners of their Lord!

Sun-happy blue jays shrieked their appreciation and their thanks. I was too full of words to speak, too full of thoughts to think. I was the only silent jay.

This was a Christmas present I had not expected, Lord, and it was wrapped exquisitely, even divinely! How could I adequately have thanked you?

Your grateful jay

Happy Birthday, Lord Jesus!
Christmas Day
December 25

If you should hear that I am giving icebergs to everybody for Christmas, pay no attention. The story has very little truth in it. How could I get several hundred icebergs, one for each of my friends and two for Catherine? And what would Catherine do with them? Use them for earrings?

Christmas, as everybody knows, is a time for the silly and the sublime. It is a time for love, and love embraces even silly things. But icebergs for Christmas? Why? God will provide plenty of ice on the roads and millions of scintillating iridescent icicles to hang from the eaves of our roofs, like so many Christmas stockings.

We spend plenty of time here in Madonna House on the silly and the sublime, on things that give joy to people. Since we are all poor, we are all beggars. We do not buy presents for one another. We make them. Sometimes with great skill, sometimes with very little skill. But always with patience and work and love.

The more you love God, the more you love your neighbor. The more you love your neighbor, the more you love God. We show our love for God by making something pretty or lovely or exquisitely beautiful, or crazy and ridiculous and absurd, and giving it to those we love with the love of God stamped into every part of it.

Some work with paper, papier-maché, linen, metal, wood, plastics, paints, water colors, crayons, pottery, candles, clay, dried flowers or anything handy. Some make up songs. Some create skits. Some write idiotic drivel (like me). Some make funny jewelry or carve comic figures for their friends. Some draw cartoons.

On Christmas Eve as the hour of glory approaches, all our preparations are finished. All is ready.

Usually many priests concelebrate Midnight Mass, and the Madonna House choir always tries to outdo the angels who sang to the shepherds so many years ago. And each priest offers three Masses during the day.

My Masses, my Christmas present to Madonna House and to all the world, will be said with great joy and will be offered for the sick and the dying, all the unfortunate and poor, all the humiliated and degraded and abused, all prisoners, all travellers, all the hopeless and despairing, and all those contemplating a better birthplace for their babies than that dirty old stable!

Lift the chalice with me. And drink from it. It will hold enough treasure to buy peace on earth and good will to everyone. It will shed a light powerful enough to guide even the blind to safety. And it will fill you all with illimitable love.

Gather with me and sing "Happy birthday, Lord Jesus; happy birthday to you."

He loved the wise men. He'll love you.

Other Books by Eddie Doherty

Broadway Murders
Captain Marooner (with Louis B. Davidson)
The Conquering March of Don Bosco
A Cricket in My Heart
Dark Masquerade (with Borden Chase)
Desert Windows
East River
Gall and Honey
A Hermit Without a Permit
I Cover God
King of Sinners
Lambs in Wolfskins
Martin
Matt Talbot
My Hay Ain't In
A Nun with a Gun
Psalms of a Sinner
The Rain Girl
The Secret of Mary (Adaptation)
Spendor of Sorrow
True Devotion to Mary (Adaptation)
Tumbleweed
Wisdom's Fool

Books Currently Available

A Cricket In My Heart
Gall and Honey: The Story of a Newspaperman
The Secret of Mary (Adaptation from Louis de Montfort)
Splendor of Sorrow: For Sinners Only
True Devotion to Mary (Adaptation from Louis de Montfort)
Tumbleweed: A Biography (of Catherine Doherty)
Wisdom's Fool (Biography of Louis de Montfort)

Available from:
Madonna House Publications
Combermere, Ontario, Canada
K0J 1L0